Mickey Mantle

The American Dream
Comes to Life®

The Companion Volume to the
Public Television Videography™ *Program Special*

by Mickey Mantle
and Lewis Early

Edited, compiled, and sequenced by Douglas A. Mackey

SPORTS PUBLISHING, L.L.C.
www.sportspublishingllc.com

Supervising editor, compiler, and sequencer: Douglas A. Mackey
Production supervision and interior design: Michelle Dressen
Dustjacket design: Michelle Dressen

Photos by the New York Yankees, *The Sporting News*, *The New York Times*, the Baseball Hall of Fame,
the National Archives, Bettman Archives/UPI, the Mickey Mantle Collection, Mark Gallagher,
Barry Halper, Raymond Gallo, and other private collectors. Every effort has been made to trace the ownership
of copyrighted photos. If we have failed to give adequate credit, we will be pleased to make changes in future printings.

ISBN: 1-58261-499-7

Printed in the United States

*This book is dedicated to the memory of Roger Maris,
as good a ballplayer and as good a man as there ever was.*

Contents

Acknowledgments

The authors wish to give special acknowledgment to the following individuals for their invaluable contributions:

Merlyn Mantle
Danny Mantle
The Mantle family
Lew Rothgeb
Richard Hall
John F. Lehr, Jr.

Douglas A. Mackey
William A. Remas and family
Joe and Peter Bannon
Lou D'Ermilio
Tom Sturdivant
Steve Janson

The authors wish to thank the following individuals and organizations for their assistance and support.

American Program Service—
  Jan Goldstein
Public Television
The New York Yankees
The New York Daily News—
  Hugo Masslich and Dave Kaplan
WABC Yankees Radio—
  Steve Appel
USA Today—
  Gene Policinski
The Associated Press
The Sporting News
Sports Illustrated—
  Stanley Weil
The National Archives
The Bettman Archives/UPI
The National Baseball Hall of Fame
Mickey Mantle's Restaurant (NY)—
  Bill Liederman
WFAN Radio (NY)
Billy Martin
Bill "Moose" Skowron
Carrie Lee Rothgeb and family
Timothy Rothgeb
Roy True and Kathy Hampton
Barry Halper
Mark Gallagher
Andy Strasberg
David Hershkowitz
John and Judy Leavitt
May Masunaga and Scott Alden
Robin Cohen and family
Jesse Raiford
Frank Gannon
Dave and Kellye Parker
President Richard Nixon
President George Bush
President Bill Clinton
Estelle Galeano & Joe Kierland
Leslie Deetken
Dr. Harry Friedman
Video Arts — Kim Salyer, Bob Johns & David Murray

The Oakland A's - Tony La Russa
Dennis and Nancy Eckersley
Jose Canseco
Cusy Canseco
Dave Henderson
Rickey Henderson
Carney and Debbie Lansford
Mark McGwire
Pete Rose
Bruce Jenkins
Bob Costas
Roy Firestone
Larry King
Tony Kornheiser
Marty Zad
Mel Allen
Sonny Slaughter
Phil Rizzuto
Paul Simon
Jay Johnstone
Steve Williams
The S.F. Giants — Ben Oakes
Tom Oakes
Rich Hebert
Randy Ottenberg
Phil and Suzie Donaldson
Chuck and Jo Clessler
Jim Stuckey and family
Barbara Stuckey
John and Jacquie Drucker
Joe and Gail DeSciose
Lynette Sonne
Hugh Andrews
Lincoln Norton
James Joyce
Tom and Kitty Kelly
Allan Kaye
Manuel Rodriguez
Ida Honesty
Dr. James Zucherman
Delmy Marquina

When in New York visit Mickey Mantle's Restaurant, 42 Central Park South, New York NY 10019 Phone: (212) 688-7777

Preface

by Lewis Early

I met Mickey Mantle for the first time when I was seven years old. The meeting took place at Griffith Stadium in Washington, D.C. The Yankees were getting ready to play the old Washington Senators.

Mickey was my idol, as he was to millions of kids across the country. I had made a wooden plaque for him, a truly awful piece of handiwork, worse than some craft project a child might bring home from summer camp. It said "MICKEY MANTLE: WORLD'S GREATEST BASEBALL PLAYER." Below those words I had painted a picture of Mickey hitting a home run that I had traced from a magazine photo.

I made my way down to the visiting dugout before the game, proudly showed my plaque to the guard and told him that I wanted to see Mr. Mantle. He studied me and my gift for a moment and then turned into the dugout and called out, "Hey Mick!"

Suddenly, overcome with anxiety, I shoved the plaque into the guard's hands and started back up the stairs toward our seats. I had taken only a few steps when a hand grabbed my shoulder and turned me around. It was the guard. He looked at me sternly and said, "Mr. Mantle wants to see you."

I was terrified. I thought, "Oh boy, I've really done it now." The guard led me back to the dugout, and I saw Mickey waiting for me. I slowly walked up to him and he asked me, "Hey, where're you goin' bud?"

I couldn't speak, but it didn't matter. Mickey reached out and shook my hand and said to me, "This is the nicest thing anybody's ever done for me. Thanks a lot. I'll really treasure it." Then he reached into the dugout, grabbed a bat and ball and handed them to me. As he did this, he asked me my name and I told him.

I turned to go back up to my seat, but Mickey stopped me. "Where're you sittin'?" he asked. I pointed to the upper deck. He looked at the guard and winked and said to him, "These seats here're empty, aren't they?" The guard winked back and said, "Yes sir, they sure are."

"Well Lew, why don't you and your friends come down and sit here by the dugout as my guests?" I couldn't believe it. My three older friends who had brought me to the game were eagerly watching from the top of the aisle. They were in awe of the fact that I was actually talking to Mickey Mantle. I waved to them and signaled for them to come down. When they arrived, I introduced them to Mickey. He spoke to all of us for a few minutes and then turned to leave. Then he stopped for a moment, looked back at me and said, "Lemme see if I can hit one out for you today."

Mickey hit two home runs that day, and drove in four runs. The Yankees won the game. (Of course, they *were* playing the Senators.) Every inning, when the Yankees came in from the field, he waved to me and my friends. It's a memory that is indelibly etched in my mind, and I remember it as if it happened yesterday.

From that time on, I made a point of going to every Yankees game in Washington. I would always go down to the dugout to say hello to Mickey before each game. Sometimes I even went over to the Shoreham Hotel and sat in the lobby until I saw him and the other players. I even went up to Yankee Stadium in New York several times. Over the years he gave me many bats and balls, most of which I still have. The ushers and guards got to know me as, "The Kid Who Knows Mickey Mantle."

The years passed, and as I grew up, I stayed in touch with Mickey. He must have told me hundreds of different stories over the years. When I became a writer, I started keeping notes on the different stories he told. I didn't do this with any particular purpose in mind. All I wanted to do was record the stories so that I could remember them later.

When the opportunity came to act as head writer for the Mantle Videography™ Program, and as co-author of this companion volume, I jumped at the chance. In some ways, it was as if I had been waiting my whole life for that opportunity.

The concept for the program was simple, yet radical: Mickey would sit in his trophy room and tell stories, which would be compiled in the first truly autobiographical program. There would be no narrator. The interviewer (me) and the interviewer's questions would neither be seen nor heard. No one else would be interviewed. It would be strictly Mantle, telling his favorite stories, with supporting archival footage, photos, and memorabilia. Period music would give the viewer a feel for the times during which the events Mickey recounted took place.

The success of the program is now well documented. It turned out exactly as we had envisioned, and hundreds of thousands, if not millions, of people have enjoyed it. No project that I have been associated with has generated as much positive commentary and correspondence. It may be titled **Mickey Mantle: The American Dream *Comes to Life*®**, but for those of us who worked on it, and to the many Mickey Mantle and baseball fans around the country, it's a dream come true.

While we were working on the program, especially during the filming at Mickey's home, I spent a great deal of time with him and his marvelous family. I must acknowledge their cooperation and support, and their warmth and hospitality. I thank them for their kindness and assistance, and most of all for their friendship. I just wish that all kids could grow up and find out that their idol is as good and as wonderful as they always dreamed that he/she would be.

One final note: On the last day of shooting, when Mickey and I had finished the interviews and the crew was stowing away equipment, I took a closer look at the walls of his trophy room. There on one wall, in the midst of his many awards, was a small wooden plaque faded by time that simply said: "MICKEY MANTLE: WORLD'S GREATEST BASEBALL PLAYER."

Introduction to Commemorative Edition

Shortly after I completed work on the first edition of this book, Mickey announced that he had voluntarily admitted himself to the residential treatment program for alcoholism at the Betty Ford Center in California, which he subsequently completed. A new chapter began in Mickey's life, a chapter that involved acknowledging his long-standing battle with alcoholism and the problems it had created in his life. His many fans and the public in general embraced his actions and showed their support for his commitment to take positive action to deal with his alcoholism. Mickey received more letters of support during his stay at Betty Ford than any other participant in the history of the center and this outpouring of love and compassion touched him deeply.

With his new sobriety he became committed to do everything possible to help raise public awareness of the detrimental effects of both alcohol and drug abuse. Prior to his stay at the Betty Ford Center Mickey's philosophy was one of, "Do as I say, not as I do." That changed dramatically afterward, and maintaining his sobriety became one of the most important issues in his life. He vowed that he would never take a drink again because, as he put it, "How could I let down all of those people who showed me so much support? How could I ever face them again?" It was a vow that he kept, and he never drank again.

Shortly after completing the program, Mickey's son Billy died of heart failure. This was a complication resulting from Hodgkin's disease, a hereditary disease that attacks the lymph system and had claimed the lives of both Mickey's father and grandfather. Mickey truly believed for most of his life that Hodgkin's disease would kill him as well, and he fully expected to die at an early age. He made no secret of the fact that his abusive lifestyle was in large part a product of his belief that he would become the next victim of Hodgkin's disease in the Mantle family. It was a cruel and ironic blow for Mickey to see the disease skip his generation only to then have it claim his son Billy. In fact, one of Mickey's most famous quotes was, "If I knew I was going to live this long, I'd have taken better care of myself." His son Billy's death was devastating to Mickey and the entire Mantle family, and thanks to his new-found sobriety, Mickey was truly there to support his loved ones when they needed him to help them through their grief.

However, his experience at the Betty Ford Center and his son Billy's death served to renew Mickey's commitment to spread the word about the dangers of alcoholism and drug abuse, and he dedicated himself to the cause. He began working to form his own foundation to better serve that cause, and was working diligently toward that end through interviews, fund raising and other means of heightening public awareness about these terrible problems.

Unfortunately, the damage inflicted by his years of drinking took its toll, and in April 1995 it was obvious that Mickey's liver had been severely impaired. The situation deteriorated quickly, and by June it became clear that he would need a liver transplant to survive. His condition was so critical that he was placed in the most urgent category of organ donor recipients, Fortunately (and miraculously to those of us unfamiliar with organ donation procedures) a liver that was a proper match became available within days, in part because of Mickey's common "O" blood type and in part through the excellent organ donor network in the Texas-Oklahoma area. The surgery was performed at Baylor University Hospital and Medical Center in Dallas and the transplant was successful.

Those of us who were close to Mickey rode a roller-coaster of emotions during those times. There was the good news of his successful alcohol rehabilitation at the Betty Ford Center, the bad news of just how serious his liver condition was and how much it had deteriorated, the realization that a transplant would be required, the hope generated by finding a suitable donor organ, the amazing success of the transplant itself. Because of the strict guideline for organ donor recipients, Mickey had in effect saved his own life by entering the Betty Ford Center and then maintaining his sobriety. One of the requirements for receiving a liver transplant is that the individual must have remained sober for at least a year prior to the transplant. So, even though he didn't realize it at the time, by successfully completing the Betty Ford program Mickey saved his life in more ways than one, for without the Betty Ford program he would never have qualified as a recipient.

Frankly, for the first few days after his liver transplant I felt like I was walking on air. I was so relieved and happy about Mickey's new lease on life from his transplant that it caused me to value my relationship with him more than ever. It was a most joyous time. As the news came forth that he was accepting the organ and his condition improved I actually felt like dancing in the street out of the sheer joy that I felt. I was not alone in that feeling.

And then, just when we felt Mickey had beaten the odds and gained a new lease on life, we learned the sad, cruel, devastating news: not only had the doctors found that Mickey had contracted cancer, but also that it was a particularly virulent strain of cancer and had spread rapidly throughout his system. Almost overnight we found ourselves moving from an ecstatic state of great hope and promise to the shock and, finally, the acceptance that Mickey was dying, quickly and inevitably, and there was nothing that could be done about it.

It was heartbreaking for us all, from the most casual fan to family members and close friends. Mickey had a way of touching people such that they took his many trials and tribulations personally. But Mickey took it all in stride, with the great dignity and composure that he had shown throughout his life and, as in so many other things, his last thoughts were of others rather than of himself. When he realized the effect he'd had on organ donor volunteers (the number of new donors skyrocketed when the news of Mickey's liver transplant was released to the media), in typical Mickey Mantle fashion he began to look for a way in which he might help others who were in similar circumstances.

To that end, the Mickey Mantle Foundation was formed. Through Mickey's inspiration, the last "Mickey Mantle Baseball Card" was created: a Mickey Mantle organ donor card that is distributed by the foundation under the auspices of the Baylor University Medical Center. These Mickey Mantle organ donor cards can be obtained by calling the Baylor University Medical Center at 1-800-477-MICK (1-800-477-6425), The call and the card are both free, but in many ways it is the most valuable Mickey Mantle baseball card of them all.

In his final days Mickey proved once again to be the hero that so many of us grew up believing in. In spite of great pain, his weakened condition and the knowledge that he was dying, he continued to think of others. For those of us who were his friends, he will always remain a hero and an inspiration to us. So please take a moment to order your Mickey Mantle organ donor card and help realize Mickey's final wish. Mickey has shown us that we all have the capability to be heroes in our own lives. All we need to do is to take a brief moment and act. So please honor Mickey's last wish, and remember what he said about becoming an organ donor: "If you really want to be a hero, be an organ donor." Mickey would be very proud of you all.

—Lewis Early, September 1995

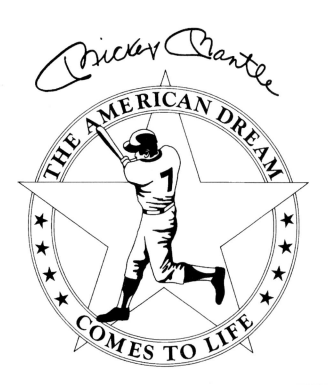

"A magnificent Yankee, the great number 7, Mickey Mantle." — Mel Allen on "Mickey Mantle Day" at Yankee Stadium, June 8, 1969.

This is me in my uniform when I played Sandlot Ball in Miami, Oklahoma. Miami was only a few miles from Commerce, where I grew up.

— I —
Introduction

Me and my Dad, Mutt Mantle. He named me after Mickey Cochrane the great catcher. I'm sure glad he didn't know Mickey's real name was Gordon!

We were always hunting and fishing when we were kids. This is me and my twin brothers, Ray & Roy, and my sister Barbara. That one fish is almost as big as Barbara!

This is me and my twin brothers, Ray & Roy. They were pretty good athletes, too.

Another one with Ray & Roy. They played for awhile in the Yankees' farm system.

Me and Ray & Roy played just about every sport. Here they're in their football uniforms. In high school, I got kicked in the shin during football practice and ended up in the hospital with osteomyelitis, a bone disease. If it wasn't for penicillin, which had just come out, I might've died or lost my leg. I was never drafted because of this disease.

This is me with my Mom. I guess everybody thinks their Mom is the greatest, and that's how I feel about her. She brought me up right, and when I hurt my leg, she was the one who kept them from amputating it. I owe her a lot.

Tom Greenwade was the Yankees scout who signed me right after I graduated from high school. He first saw me at a game where he'd gone to scout someone else. I hit a couple of home runs into the river at that game. He offered me $400 to play in Joplin for the rest of the summer. My Dad wasn't going for it, so Tom threw in a $1,100 bonus. Later he told me I was the best prospect he ever saw. This picture was taken after the Army wouldn't draft me. He's pointing at one of my injuries.

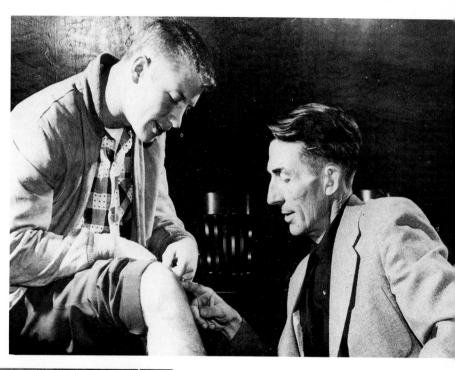

Here I'm relaxing during the off season in Oklahoma. I liked shooting pool and I wasn't too bad at it.

Me and Ray & Roy looking over one of my contracts in the off season. The first contract I signed for the big leagues was at the end of spring training in 1951. Casey Stengel called me in to meet with owners Del Webb and Dan Topping and General Manager George Weiss. Casey really stuck up for me, and got them to give me $7,500, which was $2,500 more than the minimum. It seemed like a fortune to me then. It was probably the biggest moment in my career.

Me and my wife, Merlyn, looking over a contract. I first saw Merlyn at a football game where she was a majorette. A friend set up a triple date with her and two of her friends. We got married December 23, 1951.

I was waiting in Oklahoma for the Yankees to send me my ticket and expense money for spring training in Phoenix in 1951. A reporter came to interview me when I hadn't shown up and the Yankees were trying to find me.

In 1952, they held a "Mickey Mantle Day" for me in Commerce. Folks were really proud of me.

TULSA HONORS MANTLE

Yankee Gets Griggs Trophy for Bringing Glory to Oklahoma

On "Mickey Mantle Day" in Commerce in 1952, the people lined the streets and we drove through town in a convertible.

Pitcher Ralph Terry, Scout Tom Greenwade, and me. Tom signed both Ralph and me.

This is me sliding into second for a double in my rookie year. Most people don't know it, but I wore number six when I first played with the Yankees. Cliff Mapes wore #7 for the first part of the year, but while I was in the minors, Cliff got traded to the St. Louis Browns. Bob Cerv took #7 for awhile, but he was sent down to the minors the same day I came back to the Yankees, August 22, 1951. That's when I got #7.

Me and Casey. This was taken when I first came up with the Yankees. Casey was telling everyone that I was Babe Ruth, Lou Gehrig, and Joe DiMaggio all rolled into one.

—II—
Casey & The Early Days

Joe DiMaggio was like an idol to me. I think he was probably the best all-around player ever.

When I came up to the Yankees, I joined a team that won five straight World Series. I mean, everybody talked about the Bronx Bombers because of all of the great hitters, but we had a great pitching staff, too. We had Allie Reynolds, Vic Rashi, Eddie Lopat, Whitey Ford, and Joe Page in the bullpen. It was just an unbelievable team.

I was hitting pepper one day with three guys. While we were playing, there was a guy who walked behind 'em. Well, I hit one kind of hard, and whoever was supposed to catch it didn't catch it. It hit the guy who was walking behind them in the shins, right on the leg. He turned around and looked and it was Joe DiMaggio! That was the first time I ever saw Joe DiMaggio!

I thought, "Oh My God, I've hit my man!" Because as far as I'm concerned, Joe DiMaggio is probably the greatest all-around baseball player that ever lived. And I had just hit him with the ball!

This is Casey after the Yankees won five straight World Championships, 1949-1953. I don't think any team will do that again. I remember that when I'd make an error or something in a game, one of the players would pull me aside and say "Hey, don't mess around with my money!" They *expected* to play in the World Series, and were all counting on that World Series check.

TUESDAY, SEPTEMBER 15, 1953

STENGEL AT PEAK OF 44-YEAR CAREER

First Pilot to Take 5 Flags in Row Was Once Paid for Not Managing Dodgers

Casey Stengel

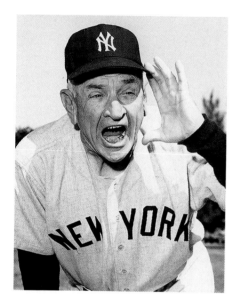

Casey was a great manager. He was one of the first to platoon his players. I think my Dad saw that coming, because he and my Grandad taught me to switch hit so I'd get to play no matter who was pitching.

Casey became almost like a father to me. He always called me "my boy." He would say "That's my boy there," you know. That's how close we became. He loved to brag to the press about me. He would tell them that I was going to be the next Babe Ruth, Lou Gehrig, and Joe DiMaggio all rolled into one.

I've told the story many times about when I got sent back down to the minor leagues in 1951. We were in Detroit at the time. We had just arrived there, and I'd just had a really terrible series up in Boston. Casey let me get dressed with the rest of the guys and go out on the field. Then he called me back into the clubhouse. He sent the clubhouse man out to get me and he brought me back in. He wanted to tell me alone, by himself.

Well, he had tears in his eyes, and, of course, it broke my heart. He told me, "You've lost all your confidence. I think it would be really good for you to go down for awhile. All we want you to do is just go to Kansas City and get a couple of home runs, a couple of hits, and the first thing you know, you'll get your confidence back, and we'll bring you right back up." Then he said, "You go ahead and get dressed and take off. I'll tell everybody what happened." I've always thought it was really nice of him to let everybody go out of the clubhouse before he told me.

The first time I got up to bat in Kansas City, I laid down a drag bunt and I got a hit. When I came into the dugout after that bunt, George Selkirk, the manager, said "Mick, we know you can bunt. The Yankees didn't send you down here to learn how to bunt. They want you to start hitting the ball so you can get your confidence back. That's the only thing you're down here for."

Me and Casey at Yankee Stadium. Casey became almost like a father to me.

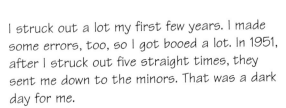

I struck out a lot my first few years. I made some errors, too, so I got booed a lot. In 1951, after I struck out five straight times, they sent me down to the minors. That was a dark day for me.

Casey used to do things when he managed that nobody understood when he did them. Most of the time they worked out. If you asked him about it afterward, he always could tell you why he did it, and it usually made sense.

I'm signing another contract with Casey looking on. He always looked after me. He used to call me "my boy."

MANTLE SENT TO MINORS

JULY 14, 1951—DETROIT—Mickey Mantle, the highly regarded rookie outfielder signed by the Yankees earlier this year, was sent down to the Yankees AAA minor league team in Kansas City yesterday. The 19-year-old Mantle has struggled over the past month, seeing his batting average drop from a May 16 high of .308 to his current .261. He reached a new plateau of frustration in Boston when he struck out five consecutive times in the Memorial Day doubleheader against the Red Sox.

When asked if Mantle was through, manager Casey Stengel snapped, "You wish you were through like that kid's through."

Stengel insisted that the move is temporary. "He's been trying to do too much, putting too much pressure on himself. He's striking out too much. He just needs to get his batting eye back, which I'm confident he'll do in Kansas City." Stengel then predicted that Mantle would be back with the team before the season is finished.

Stengel has touted Mantle as the successor to the great Joe DiMaggio. While Mantle has shown flashes of brilliance, particularly with several spectacular home run blasts, he has been mired in a terrible slump over the past month. He leaves the team with seven home runs, 45 RBIs, and a .261 batting average.

Me with my Dad and Cliff Mapes at the lead mines in Oklahoma. Cliff played outfield for the Yankees too. I'll tell you, I'm glad I made it in baseball. Mining is a hard life.

"I Thought I Raised A Ballplayer!"

Casey was true to his word and brought me back up from the minors later in the '51 season. This picture was taken just after I came up. You can see how happy I was.

After that bunt I didn't get a hit for, like, 22 straight times at bat. I had really reached the bottom. I felt so bad I called my Dad in Commerce, Oklahoma from my hotel room. Commerce is only about 150 miles from Kansas City. I said "Dad, I don't think I can make it. I just can't play ball anymore. Won't you come and get me?"

He asked me where I was and I told him. He said, "I'll be there in a little bit." He drove all the way from Commerce to the hotel in Kansas City. He got there in about three or four hours. He knocked on the door and I let him in, and he got my suitcase and started throwing stuff in it. I said, "What are you doing?" He said, "Well, I'm taking you home." I said, "What do you mean, you're taking me home?" He said, "You said you can't play baseball anymore, so you might as well come on back with me."

Then he said, "I thought I raised a man. You're nothing but a coward. A quitter." I thought he'd come up and pat me on the back and start saying, "Hey, hang in there," or something like that. Instead he really let me have it for about five minutes, calling me a coward and a quitter. He said, "You might as well be a miner like me, so just get your stuff and let's get ready to go." It took me about five minutes to talk him into letting me have another shot at it.

After he left, I went on a tear you couldn't believe. I ended up hitting about .360 or so the rest of the time I was there, and had about 10 or 15 home runs and 60 RBIs. It was unbelievable the way I started hitting. So whatever he did, it was the right thing. And sure enough, later that season the Yankees brought me back up.

Bill Gallo is a famous sports cartoonist. He drew a cartoon of Billy Martin, me and Whitey Ford in the *NY Daily News*. We were sort of like the "Dead End Kids" or something.

The King Solomon Story

Another time I'll never forget was when Casey called me and Billy and Whitey into his office. We were starting to get a reputation, even in the press. For example, Gallo, the *Daily News* cartoonist, came out with one of his cartoons. It showed me and Billy and Whitey standing in front of Casey, and Casey was dressed up like a judge behind the bench, and we were standing there and Billy's got a BB gun behind his back, I've got a sling shot and Whitey had a pea shooter behind him, like the Dead End Kids or somebody like that. And Casey was bawling us out.

About that same time was when Casey called us into his office. He could scare you. I mean, he could get really serious. This time he said, "Do you guys know who King Solomon was?" And we all went, no, not really. We were looking at each other trying to figure out what he was talking about.

He said, "Well, King Solomon was a guy that had a hundred wives, and they couldn't all live in the same house with him, so they had to be scattered all around town. But if he's got all these wives," he said, "he couldn't go get 'em, so he had a guy that lived with him that would run and get the wives and bring 'em to him if he wanted one. Even if he had one way across town that he wanted, this guy had to run and get her and bring her to him. No matter what time of night, even if it was two or three o'clock in the morning, this guy had to run and get her."

"King Solomon lived to be a hundred years old," he said. "Do you know how old this guy that was running and getting King Solomon's wives was when he died? He was 30 years old."

We were all looking at each other. Then he said, "Don't you know what that proves? That just proves that it's not the women that kill you. It's that running after them that does it!"

Stan Musial was my first idol. This was when we were getting ready to testify to the Kefauver Committee. They called me and Stan as well as Ted Williams and Casey Stengel to testify.

Casey loved to talk. He could really get you going with his "Stengelese." This is when he testified to the Kefauver Committee. He talked for a long time, but I don't think anybody really understood what he said.

The Kefauver Committee

There was a Senate Committee in Washington called the Kefauver Committee and they were trying to prove that baseball was anti-trust or something like that. I never did know what it was, but I was scared to death. They had asked Casey, owner Del Webb, and myself to come from the Yankees, and they had Stan Musial and Ted Williams come too.

We went down there the night before, and we got up early the next morning. All the way on the trip down there, Del Webb was just saying, "Hey, relax," because I was really scared. I was afraid I was going to get thrown in prison or something. I didn't know.

When we got there, the first guy that they swore in was Casey. They asked him, did he think that baseball should be exempt from anti-trust laws or whatever it was, whatever the question was. He started by saying: "I started playing baseball in Kankakee, Illinois, back in 1890," or whatever he said. I really don't know what it was. He talked for about an hour and a half or so — he was really putting the Stengelese to 'em that day.

Casey Stengel (Excerpt from actual testimony): "Well, I'll tell you, I got a little concerned yesterday in the first three innings when I saw that my three players that I'd gotten rid of, I said, well, if I lose nine what am I gonna do? And when I had a couple of my players that I thought so great of that didn't do so good up to the sixth inning, I was more confused, but I finally had to go and call on a young man in Baltimore that we don't own, and the Yankees don't own him, and he's doing pretty good and I would actually have to tell you that I think we're more the Greta Garbo

type now from success. We are being hated, I mean from the ownership and all, we are being hated. Every sport that gets too great or one individual . . . ”

They finally asked him to step down. Then they swore me in. I was the next witness. Senator Kefauver said, “Mister Mantle, what do you think? Do you think baseball should be exempt from anti-trust laws?” or whatever. I said, “Sir, I don't really know that much about it, but everything that Casey said, I agree with.” And everybody laughed. Then he said, “Mister Mantle, would you mind telling us what Mister Stengel said?” And everyone laughed again.

I got called to testify right after Casey. I was really scared. I thought they might try to put me in jail or something!

Casey getting ready to testify to the Kefauver Committee. He could go on for hours if there was someone there to listen. The sportswriters loved him. When he left the Yankees they had a special dinner for him. I don't think they'd ever done that before.

Senate Investigates Baseball's Antitrust Status

JULY 10, 1958, WASHINGTON— Yesterday the Senate's Antitrust Committee, chaired by Senator Estes Kefauver (Dem., Tenn.) conducted hearings looking into Major League Baseball's exemption from anti-trust legislation. Among those called to testify to the committee were baseball stars Ted Williams, Stan Musial, and Mickey Mantle. New York Yankees owner Del Webb and Manager Casey Stengel also testified.

The highlight of the hearing was Mr. Stengel's testimony, which lasted over an hour. A spellbound, yet highly amused audience listened as Mr. Stengel took them through a circuitous history of major and minor league baseball, the trials and tribulations of managing, offering such unusual commentary as comparing the New York Yankees to Greta Garbo. (see "Kefauver Committee" page 26)

A lot of people don't remember it, but Billy Martin was a pretty good ballplayer, especially when it really counted. His lifetime World Series average was well over .300. One time Harry Byrd, a real hard thrower with the Philadelphia Athletics, was pitching against us. He was getting guys out by pitching inside. Casey told us, "I'll give a hundred bucks to anybody for each time he can get hit by a pitch." Billy got hit three times!

Whitey, me, and Billy. Whitey won this game just after he'd gotten back from the Army. I drove in Billy with the winning run. Here we're celebrating in the clubhouse afterward. Me and Billy and Whitey were as close as friends could be.

— III —
Billy & Whitey

I think Whitey Ford was as good a pitcher as there was. I'll tell you, if the World Series was on the line, I'd give the ball to Whitey every time.

Another question that I get asked a lot is, "What was Billy Martin really like?" I guess people ask me this because me and Billy were such close friends. In fact, I have three brothers, and none of them were any closer to me than Billy was.

Billy was always a great one for jokes. He loved to pull a joke on somebody. He'd get a bigger kick out of that than anybody that I've ever played with.

During my first year with the Yankees, Joe DiMaggio would come to the ballpark in a suit and tie every day. We'd come out in Levis and tennis shoes or anything like that. But Joe was always well dressed.

Billy had one of those prank pens that would spill ink when you went to use it. He'd run up to Joe and ask, "Joe, would you sign this ball for me?" When Joe opened the pen and went to use it, ink would spill all over him. And Joe would grumble, "Oh Billy, how could you have done that?"

The first time I met Whitey was when he married Joanie before the '51 season. It was after our last exhibition game, which was at Ebbets Field in Brooklyn. We all got in buses and went to the wedding. Whitey was in the service then, so I didn't get to know him until he came back later.

This is Whitey, me, and Billy (back row) after we'd gone deep sea fishing. We used to do everything together.

"Whiskey Slick"

Here's "Slick" in action. Usually, when he really needed to get someone out, he could do it.

*T*he first time I met Whitey Ford was in 1951. I remember that we were playing a couple of exhibition games against the Brooklyn Dodgers before the season. Whitey was going to marry Joanie. After one of the games they had a bus to take everybody to Whitey's wedding.

Casey was a great manager. He really knew how to talk to his players. Once we had lost four straight games and he called a clubhouse meeting. Me and Billy and Whitey had probably been partying a little too much. We might've missed a bus or two or been late getting in at night or something.

Casey had a knack of getting on the guys who were going good. We were probably going pretty good at that time, and some of the other guys weren't doing so well. We were kind of his pets, you know, "teacher's pets." After he had gotten on us in front of everybody, as he would walk out, he kind of gave us that wink, like, don't worry about it, you've done all right.

He started the meeting that day by going on about how we needed to get to the ballpark earlier, that guys who weren't hitting too well should come out early for extra hitting, and players should take more infield practice and shag more fly balls. He started getting more serious as he went on with his talk.

Suddenly, he looked right at me and Billy and Whitey and he said, "I'll tell you something else. Some of you guys are getting 'Whiskey Slick.'"

Well nobody had ever heard that expression before, but everybody knew who he was talking about. He went ahead with the meeting, and at the end of the meeting he said, "I'll tell you another thing: Some of you milkshake drinkers better snap out of it, too!"

From that time on, everybody started calling me and Whitey "Slick." And we've called each other "Slick" ever since then. I don't know how come the name didn't stick to Billy. He was just as bad as the two of us, but for some reason or other they just called me and Whitey "Slick." Eventually, it became just Whitey's nickname.

Whitey with some of the guys who served with him in the Army. He missed all of the '51 and '52 seasons.

Casey's the one who gave Whitey the nickname "Slick."

Billy loved to play jokes. One time I got a death threat. The guy said that if I played in Boston he would shoot me. Even the FBI got involved. The FBI told me to stay away from the hotel room windows. Billy waited until I was by a window, and then pulled up the blinds and yelled "Look out! Get down!" I dove under the bed. Billy laughed like crazy. But at the ballpark he said, "I'll wear your number and you can wear mine." Nothing scared Billy.

Me and Billy were roommates when he was with the Yankees. Can you
imagine players nowadays carrying their own suitcases?

The Kenmore Hotel Story

I remember that, one day in Boston, we had a day game, and me and Billy Martin went out to a restaurant to eat dinner afterward. The next thing we knew it was about ten 'til twelve, and we had a midnight curfew. But we thought if we really hurried we could make it.

Well, we got stuck in traffic, and we got back to the Kenmore Hotel where the team was staying at about five after twelve. We ran up the steps to the front door and there was Casey Stengel in the lobby with about ten or twelve writers. Casey loved to talk to the writers. He could go on all night.

So we went around back, but the door was locked. But the transom, about a story up, was open. Billy said, "If you get me up on your shoulders I could jump up and get into that window, and then I'll come around and open the door for you."

I had on a brand new sharkskin suit and I really liked it. There he was crawling all over me. I had to stand on one of the trash cans in the back alley to get him up on my shoulders to get him into the window.

He got up into the window, and came around to the door. I could hear him inside, trying to open the door. Then I didn't hear him for awhile. All of a sudden I saw him back up at the window and he said, "Hey, Mick, listen, that door's got a chain and lock on it. I can't get it open. I'll see you tomorrow."

I was still standing out in the alley, all alone. I had to stack all those trash cans up and try and get up on them to get into that window. I must have fallen off about four or five times. That sharkskin suit had lettuce and all kinds of garbage all over it.

Finally I got into the window. When I got to the room, Billy was in there already asleep!

Here's Billy hugging shortstop Phil Rizzuto after Billy drove in the winning run in the bottom of the ninth in Game 6 of the '53 World Series. It won the Series for us, the Yankees' fifth straight World Championship. It was Billy's twelfth hit in the Series. Phil went on to become a Yankees broadcaster.

Billy and me did everything together. He used to come live with me during the off season. I remember one time in Oklahoma he left all of his clothes and things in his car when we went to a club one night. He was going to lock his car, but I told him, "Aw, you don't have to do that around here." When we came out all of his stuff was stolen!

Most people think of Billy as a manager, and he was a great one. I'll tell you, he could get guys to run through a wall for him.

Whitey had some great years with the Yankees. His lifetime record was 236 wins against 106 losses. He'd have won a lot more games if he hadn't spent those years in the Army.

Roger Maris, Willie Mays, and me at an All-Star Game. Willie hit something like .400 lifetime off of Whitey, but Whitey did find a way to get him out one particular time.

The Horace Stoneham All Star Game Story

*T*his story's about after the Giants moved to San Francisco and they had the All Star game there. Everyone remembers that game because Stu Miller was blown off the mound. But I remember it for a different reason.

Whitey always seemed to have a terrible time getting Willie Mays out. I think Willie's lifetime batting average was over .400 against Whitey.

Me and Whitey went out to San Francisco a little early. We got there the day before the All Star game. We wanted to go play golf, so Whitey called Horace Stoneham, the owner of the Giants, and asked him if we could play at his country club. He said, "Sure, just sign for everything. In fact, I'll tell you what I'll do. You just sign for everything and if you get Willie out in the All Star game tomorrow, I'll take care of everything. If you don't, you'll have to pay for it."

Well, we ran up a bill of like $400 or something like that. In 1961 that was really a lot of money. So I told Whitey, "Man, if you get Willie out tomorrow, I'll buy your dinner or anything you want."

Sure enough, Whitey, I think, threw Willie a spitter or something and struck him out. It was one of the few times he ever got Willie out. It was the last out of the inning, too, and everybody said I was jumping up in the air in the outfield. I came running off the field, and grabbed Whitey like it was the last out of a World Series. Nobody could figure it out but Horace Stoneham.

Here we are at the famous "Copacabana" night club on May 15, 1957. That was quite a night.

MAY 17, 1957

YANKEE IS LINKED TO FIGHT IN CAFE

But Hank Bauer Denies That He Took a Swing at Fan in Copacabana 'Incident'

The Copacabana Incident

You know, everybody asks me about Billy Martin, but the truth is, I never saw him fight. I never saw Billy have a fight.

One of the stories that everybody wants to know about, it seems, is the old Copacabana incident. On Billy's birthday in 1957, Whitey Ford and I gave him a birthday party. We'd invited a group of Yankees and their wives.

We went to Danny's Hideaway, which was Billy's favorite place. We had dinner there, and when we finished we decided to go down and catch the ten o'clock show at the Copa with Sammy Davis. They gave us a big table in the middle of the room.

Later, two bowling teams arrived, and they were already feeling pretty good. They got to talking loud and getting on Sammy, and I think Hank Bauer said, "Hey come on, you guys, cool it. We've got our wives here and you're embarrassing them."

Well, one thing led to another and somebody said, "Meet us in the cloak room." Of course you didn't have to tell Billy but once, and Hank also. So the next thing I knew, the cloak room was full of people and everybody was swinging and throwing punches.

Suddenly there was a guy laying right at my feet. I was in the back just watching everything. I never hit anybody or got hit. But somebody had hit a guy, because he was laying at my feet. I thought it was Billy at first. I picked his head up and saw it wasn't Billy, so I dropped him back down.

The next day the headlines were "Yankees in Copa Fight" and "Billy Martin" this and that. As soon as we got to the ballpark, Billy started packing his bags. I said, "What're you doin'?" He said, "I'm gone. George Weiss (then Yankees General Manager) is just looking for a chance to get rid of me."

Mr. Weiss had warned us a few times about missing planes and trains and stuff like that. Sure enough, Billy got traded. But before that, I'll tell you one of the funniest parts of the whole thing.

One of the guys who'd been in the fight sued Hank Bauer, and we all had to go to court. I'd never been in court before, so I was pretty nervous.

They asked Hank and Whitey and Billy questions, and then they called me to testify. I was sitting there and the judge asked me, "Mr. Mantle, do you have gum in your mouth?" I said, "Yes sir."

I was scared to death. I didn't know what was goin' on. The judge said to me, "Would you do something with it?" I didn't know what to do with it, so I took it out of my mouth and just stuck it under the witness chair.

Then the judge said to me, "Would you tell us what happened?" I said, "Well, I don't know, your honor. I was standing in the back of the cloak room when I saw this guy laying at my feet. I picked him up and it looked like Roy Rogers had ridden through on Trigger, and Trigger had kicked him in the face." Everybody in the courtroom laughed, and the judge said, "Case dismissed."

YANKEES INVOLVED IN COPACABANA INCIDENT

MAY 16, 1957—NEW YORK— Several members of the New York Yankees baseball team reportedly were involved in a fight at the famed Copacabana night club last night here in New York. Players alleged to be involved include Billy Martin, Whitey Ford, Yogi Berra, Hank Bauer, Mickey Mantle and Johnny Kucks.

An eyewitness reported that a group of bowlers had come to the club in a rowdy mood and began shouting obscenities at Sammy Davis, Jr., who was performing at the club. The players had asked the bowlers to stop, whereupon they were challenged to meet the bowling team in the cloakroom to settle their differences.

Police are investigating, but no charges have been filed. Neither the Copacabana nor the New York Yankees could be reached for comment. Witnesses are being questioned (See "Copa Brawl" page 32)

Me, Billy, Hank & Charlene Bauer after Hank won the lawsuit against him. Even though Hank was the one who got sued, Yankees General Manager George Weiss took it out on Billy.

Casey and Billy were real close, too. After Billy got traded they didn't talk to each other for a long time. They did finally make up, though.

YANKEES MAKE BIG TRADE WITH KANSAS CITY

JUNE 15, 1957, KANSAS CITY— New York officials announced that an eight-player trade has been completed with the Kansas City Athletics. In exchange for second baseman Billy Martin, outfielder/utilityman Woodie Held, pitcher Ralph Terry and outfielder Bob Martyn, the Yankees acquired pitcher Ryne Duren, outfielder Jim Pisoni, second baseman Milt Graff and utilityman Harry Simpson.

The trade came as something of a surprise because it involved fan favorite Billy Martin and the highly regarded Ralph Terry. Yankees officials refused to comment on speculation that Martin may have been traded because of his involvement in the Copacabana night club brawl on May 15th. "We've been watching Ryne Duren," said Yankees General Manager George Weiss, "and we think he can help our pitching staff considerably. We need more (see "Trade" page 28)

Billy was like a brother to me. No one was ever closer. He was my best friend.

Billy Gets Traded

When Billy got traded to Kansas City, it just tore us up. Me and Billy and Whitey were crying and everything. It really was like losing a brother.

Later on that season, Billy was traded to Kansas City. Even though Billy expected it, when they traded Billy, it really tore us up. That was one of the blackest days of my life. We were crying on each other's shoulders and everything. Billy had been my only roommate since I came to the Yankees. So me and Billy and Whitey went out that night planning to souse it up.

I remember that Whitey was pitching the next day, and at one point he said, "I've got to go to bed, because I'm pitching tomorrow." Then he turned to Billy and said, "But I'll tell you what, if I stand straight up tomorrow when I get ready to pitch, it's gonna be a fast ball. If I bend over, it's gonna be a curve ball. But don't go and hit a home run off me." Billy said to Whitey, "Aw, don't worry, don't worry."

Sure enough, Whitey threw him either a fast ball or a slow curve, I really don't remember which it was, but Billy knew what was coming, and I'll be darned if Billy didn't hit a home run. All the way around the bases, he was laughing like hell. The next time Billy was up, Whitey knocked him down!

I've always loved to go hunting. Here I am with my
rifle and my hunting dog.

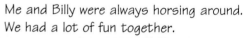

Me and Billy were always horsing around.
We had a lot of fun together.

Billy Shot a Cow

Another question people always seem to ask me is "What made Billy such a good manager?" I always tell them it's because Billy's players knew that if Billy told them to jump off a roof, that Billy would jump off with them. I even have a story to illustrate that point.

When Billy was managing the Texas Rangers, he did such a good job that after the season they gave Billy a new rifle. He wanted to go hunting with it right away. So I told him, "Well, I'll take you hunting. I know a guy with a ranch outside of San Antonio. He's a doctor and a friend of mine, and I think he'll let us hunt on his ranch. But you'll have to get up at four in the morning, because it takes hours to drive there."

Billy said, "I don't care. I want to go deer hunting with my new rifle." So we drove down there and when we got there I said, "You wait in the car and I'll go ask if it's all right for us to go hunting." I went and knocked on the door. The doctor came to the door and said, "Hey, Mick, what are you doing down here?" I said, "I've got Billy Martin out in the car with me. We're wondering if we could go deer hunting on your ranch?"

He said, "Aw, sure, Mick, anytime." I started to walk off, but he said, "By the way, will you do me a favor?" I said, "What's that?" He said, "You see that old mule standing by the barn?"

I looked over by the barn and saw this poor old mule on its last legs. Then the doctor asked me, "Would you shoot that mule for me?" I said, "Aw, Doc, we don't want to shoot your mule. We came down here to hunt deer."

He said to me, "Mick, you'd be doing me a big favor because I just don't have the heart for it. I've had him for about twenty years. He hasn't done any work for at least ten. He's old and suffering. I'm going to have to have him put away. You'd really be doing me a big favor." So I said, "Okay, we'll shoot the mule for you."

Front: Gil McDougald, Jim McDonald, and Gene Woodling. Back: Billy Martin and me. This was after Game 5 of the 1953 World Series when we beat the Dodgers 11-7. Gil McDougald, Billy Martin, and Gene Woodling all homered and I hit a grand slam. Jim McDonald was the winning pitcher.

As I was walking back to the car I thought, "I'm going to pull a joke on Billy." I ran out to the car and yanked the door open and said, "Give me my rifle!" Billy said, "What's the matter?" I said, "We drove four hours to get down here to go deer hunting, and now this guy won't let us. I'm going to shoot his mule!"

Billy said, "Oh, my God, don't do that!" He was trying to grab my rifle back, saying, "We'll get in trouble and go to jail and everything." I said, "Give me the rifle." I finally wrestled the rifle away from him and I ran out to the barn.

Pow! I shot the mule right in the neck. The mule fell over and then, right behind me, I heard, "Bam! Bam! Bam!" I turned around and there was Billy with his gun.

I said, "Billy, what are you doing? He said, "I got three of his cows!"

Billy, Eddie Lopat, and me after me and Billy homered in a '53 World Series game. Eddie'd won the game. He was 4-1 lifetime in the World Series.

Billy and me at Yankee Stadium. We were friends right up until he died. He was a heck of a guy.

1956 was probably my best year. Everything just kind of came together for me. Here I'm getting the "Sultan of Swat" award.

MANTLE WINS TRIPLE CROWN

OCT. 1, 1956-BOSTON— Mickey Mantle became the first player in nine years to win baseball's Triple Crown, and only the sixth player in history. Mantle finished the season with a final batting average of .353, 52 home runs, and 130 RBIs. He led both leagues in each of the categories, becoming only the fourth player in history to do so.

Mantle finished the season in a dramatic duel with Ted Williams in Boston, where the Yankees played their final series of the regular season. Williams finished the year with an average of .345. Williams is the only player to have won the Triple Crown twice.

When asked how he felt about winning the Triple (see "Triple Crown" page 8)

Here's Casey crowning me with the "Triple Crown," which I won in 1956. On the bats you can see my stats: 52 home runs, 130 RBIs and a .353 batting average.

In this one, I'm sliding in safe at home. Everybody was always talking about my bad legs and all, but it never stopped me from running and sliding when I needed to.

*M*ickey Mantle (from a 1956 early season interview when asked about breaking Babe Ruth's home run record): "I think that this year I'd rather lead the league in home runs, runs batted in, and hitting, and that's my goal for this year."

When I first came up there was so much pressure that was brought on me by the media and Casey bragging about me. Like I said, everybody was expecting Babe Ruth and Lou Gehrig and Joe DiMaggio all rolled into one. And it just didn't happen. A lot of people gave me a real hard time at first.

I got booed a lot in Yankee Stadium, because I didn't really do as good as Joe DiMaggio until 1956. He used to hit .323 or .330 every year, and he's probably the greatest living baseball player. So I was trying to take his place, and I wasn't doing it.

Finally, in 1956, I won the Triple Crown, but it wasn't that easy. I remember that the Yankees went into Boston for the last three games of the season. Me and Ted Williams were both hitting .348 or something like

I was always a good bunter. Here I'm laying down a drag bunt. I got a couple of bunt hits at the end of 1956 when Ted Williams and I were both trying to win the Batting Title. I bunted because I wanted to make sure I won.

that. Of course, I got a couple of bunt hits to protect my average. I was gonna make sure I got some hits. But I hit a couple of other balls pretty good, so it wasn't just the bunts that won me the title.

I think Ted was kinda upset about losing the title. Mostly I think the two bunt hits were what really made him mad. I ended up hitting .353, and I'm not sure what he ended up hitting that year, but he wasn't very far behind me. I remember that they asked him after it was over, "What do you think about Mantle out hitting you?" He said, "If I could run like him, I'd hit .400 every year!" (Mickey laughs.)

In 1956, I won the Batting Title. I hit .353. In this picture they're giving me the certificate and a silver bat. Al Kaline (left) had won the Title the year before. He'd hit .340.

Casey, Lee MacPhail, me and George Weiss signing my contract in 1957.

On Opening Day in Washington, April 17, 1956, President Eisenhower threw out the first ball. I hit two home runs that day.

TUESDAY, OCTOBER 9, 1956

LARSEN BEATS DODGERS IN PERFECT GAME; FIRST WORLD SERIES NO-HITTER GIVES YANKS 3-2 LEAD

Yogi Berra celebrating with Don Larsen after Larsen pitched his perfect game in the '56 World Series. That was one of the biggest games I ever played in.

LARSEN MASTERPIECE—A PERFECT GAME!

First World Series No-Hitter Gives Yanks Lead

OCT. 9, 1956, NEW YORK— Don Larsen made baseball history yesterday by throwing the first perfect game and no-hitter in World Series history, defeating the Brooklyn Dodgers by a score of 2-0. The victory gave the Yankees a three games to two lead in the Series. The two Yankees runs scored on Mickey Mantle's solo home run to right field with two outs in the fourth inning and Hank Bauer's RBI single in the sixth.

Larsen needed little help in shutting out the Dodgers, throwing only 97 pitches. Two defensive plays were key to preserving the no-hitter. In the second inning, Jackie Robinson hit a hard shot that deflected off third baseman Andy Carey's glove to shortstop Gil McDougal, whose strong throw barely nipped Robinson at first. Later, in the fifth inning, Gil Hodges hit a tremendous sinking line drive about 430 feet into left-center field. Mickey Mantle raced after the ball, lunging at the last second to make a spectacular backhanded catch.

Dodger pitcher Sal Maglie pitched almost as well, retiring the (see "Larsen's Perfect Game" page 3.)

The Perfect Game

"Gooney Bird" Don Larsen. During his perfect game he kept trying to talk to everybody about his no-hitter. Ballplayers are real superstitious about that, so nobody wanted to talk to him.

I guess one of the biggest games I ever played in was in the World Series against the Dodgers in 1956, in Don Larsen's perfect game. I remember that in that game, Sal Maglie was pitching a great game for the Dodgers, too.

I'm not sure if I got the first hit or not, but I know that I hit a home run off of Maglie that was right down the right field line and just barely went around the foul pole in Yankee Stadium. It said 296 feet on the outfield wall, but it went further than that. It was hit good enough that it would have been a home run in most ballparks.

Later on, we scraped another run in when someone, I think it was Hank Bauer, got on, and Andy Carey hit a double, something like that. So we scored two runs in the game. Then oh, along about that time was when we started thinking about a no-hitter.

The funny thing about the game, that I remember more than anything else, is that during the game, Larsen was trying to talk to everybody about the no-hitter. Baseball players have a superstition: If a pitcher is pitching a no-hitter, you don't say anything about it. I was down in the corner getting a drink of water and he came over to me. "Gooney Bird" is what we called him, and he said, "Hey Mickey," and I said, "What Gooney?" He said, "Wouldn't it be something if I pitched a no-hitter?" I said, "Come on man, get out of here!" I didn't want to talk about it.

Don Larsen pitching his perfect game in the '56 World Series. That was on October 8, 1956.

Another thing I remember about that game was that I made one of the best catches I've ever made. I wasn't known to be a great fielder or anything, but I could really run, you know, fast. Gil Hodges was at bat and I remember that he hit a ball that would have been way up in the upper deck at Brooklyn's Ebbet's Field. He probably hit it about 450 feet into left center field. It was right at the warning track. But Yankee Stadium was really big in center field, so there was a lot more room than in most ballparks. I had to run a long way, but I caught it. It was one of the best catches I ever made, and it saved his no-hitter.

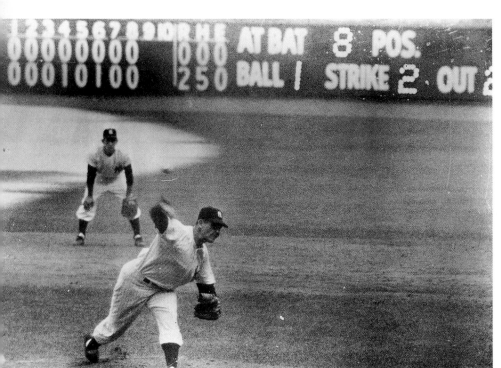

Gooney's last pitch was a called third strike to Dale Mitchell. The scoreboard tells the story.

I made one of my best catches ever in that game. Gil Hodges hit a long drive to left center. I really had to run a long way to get it. It saved Larsen's no-hitter.

Casey and Larsen after the game in the locker room. People forget that Sal Maglie had pitched a great game for the Dodgers. That day Gooney was better.

Gil McDougald, Gooney Bird, and me after his perfect game. I'd hit a home run to drive in the first run of the game. Gil made a great throw to get Jackie Robinson out in the 2nd inning.

Jensen Quits Baseball at Age 32
Refuses to Fly to Games

This is Jackie Jensen. Jackie hated to fly. He wasn't the only one. Once we were in a bad storm over the Great Lakes. It was pretty rough. I'm not sure, but I think it was John Blanchard who got scared. He told the stewardess "Put the plane down! Put the plane down!" The stewardess said, "But sir, we can't land, we're over water." John said, "Go ahead and put it down anyway. I can swim, but I can't fly!"

Jackie Jensen: The Fear of Flying

One year after the season was over, the Yankees went to Japan. Jackie Jensen was scared to death of flying. I mean, even if we were just flying from New York to Boston, much less from San Francisco to Guam to Japan. He used to have to go to a hypnotist, to be able get on an airplane, he was so scared.

On this flight, we had taken off and oh, I guess we were about two hours into the flight and we got into a storm. Of course, Jackie was up in the front of the plane in his trance. I guess he was just relaxing, because he was about half asleep.

Billy Martin was in the back of the plane and we did get into some rough weather and were bouncing around a lot. You've got to know that Jackie was a little bit out of it. The hypnotist had done a good job, I guess. Anyway, Billy put on a Mae West vest, which airplanes had in those days, and he let the air into it - Phhttt! Then he put on an oxygen mask and he went running up front and he grabbed Jackie and shouted, "Jackie! Jackie! Get up! Get up! We're goin' down!"

Of course, the plane was in a storm. It was jumping up and down and going side to side. Jackie jumped up. He was trying to get his vest and his oxygen mask and everything on. All of sudden he looked around. He saw that nobody else was moving, except Billy. It really made Jackie mad when he figured out what Billy'd done. He chased Billy all around the plane trying to catch him. They finally had to stop him, so he never did get back at him.

Here's me and Red Patterson, the Yankees publicity guy. Legend has it that he measured my home run at Griffith Stadium in Washington that I hit on April 17, 1953. It went 565 feet. Red's the one who created the "Tape Measure" home run.

SATURDAY, APRIL 18, 1953

MANTLE'S 565-FOOT HOME RUN HELPS YANKEES WIN

7-3 Defeat of Senators Features Towering Drive by Yank Slugger

This is a diagram of the home run I hit at Griffith Stadium on April 17, 1953. It went where they've marked the picture with the letter "C."

— V —
Memorable Home Runs

The Griffith Stadium Home Run

Another home run at Yankee Stadium. Everybody talked about the short porch in right field, but they forget that center field was 461 feet deep. I think Joe DiMaggio alone probably lost at least 10 home runs a year because of that. He'd hit a long shot to center that would've gone out just about anywhere else. As he came into second he'd see the ball caught way out by the monuments and he'd kick the base in disgust.

When I think about the longest ball or the hardest ball I ever hit, the one that they talk about all the time was the one in Washington at Griffith Stadium that went 565 feet.

Griffith Stadium, in case you don't know, was not like these brand new ballparks. It wasn't three decks and didn't have a dome on it or anything. It was one of the real old ballparks. The wind always seemed to blow out. But it wasn't an easy ballpark to hit home runs in because in right field there was about a ninety foot wall. In center field behind the wall there were some trees where only Larry Doby and myself had hit home runs. I hit two into those trees one year on opening day against Camilo Pascual. So it was not an easy ballpark to hit in.

I remember that Chuck Stobbs was pitching, and I hit the ball real high. There was about a thirty- or forty-mile-an-hour tail wind that day, and it went over the

This home run, #521, off of Tiger pitcher Earl Wilson, tied me with Ted Williams for fourth on the All-Time home run list. The date was April 26, 1968, and we won 5-0.

Joe Pepitone congratulates me after home run #523 on May 30, 1968. This was the first of two home runs I hit that day. It was against the Washington Senators. I went five for five, scored three runs, and had five RBIs. I was playing first base then.

auxiliary scoreboard in left field. It was a long shot. Red Patterson, the Yankees PR man, measured it. It went 565 feet.

The funny thing about the home run is that I had a terrible habit of running around the bases with my head down, because I didn't want to embarrass the pitcher. I knew he was embarrassed enough already. Especially one that long. As I came around second base I was heading to third with my head down. I heard Frank Crosetti, the third base coach, holler, "Hey, look out!" And I looked up and saw Billy Martin, who was on third when I hit the ball. He was tagged up like it was only a long fly, and I almost ran into him. He ran on in to the plate, laughing, with me right behind him. Later he told me, "That's the longest ball I've ever seen hit."

But I think I hit two or three balls harder than that. I know I hit a ball one time over the monuments in the old Yankee Stadium, up into the center field black seats. That was a long shot.

Then there was the one at USC, at Bovard Field during an exhibition game. I think that one went over six hundred feet. The USC ball park wasn't really that big. When the ball went over the fence, I was already going around second, so I didn't see how far it went. It went across a football field too, that was adjacent to the baseball field. And I hit one in San Francisco too, where they said that only DiMaggio had hit one before.

MANTLE CLOUTS TREMENDOUS HOME RUN

565-Foot Blast Clears Griffith Stadium
Yankees Swarm Nats 7-3

APR. 18, 1953, WASHINGTON— Yankee center fielder Mickey Mantle hit a tremendous home run that may well be the longest ball ever hit. His mammoth wallop came in the fifth inning off Washington pitcher Chuck Stobbs. The ball caromed over the top of the 60-foot auxiliary scoreboard in deep left field and landed several houses away from the ballpark (see photo). Billy Martin was on third base when Mantle launched his spectacular shot.

Yankees Publicity Director Red Patterson immediately left the park and found the ball in the hands of 10-year-old Donald Dunaway, who showed him where the ball had landed. Red then measured the distance, an astonishing 565 feet. Many players wondered afterward just how far the ball would have gone had it not hit the scoreboard. Senators Manager Bucky Harris said "I just wouldn't have believed a ball could be hit that hard. I've never seen anything like it."

During pre-game batting practice, Mantle put on an electrifying show. He hammered several drives deep into the right (see "Mantle's Historic Homer" page C-2)

Bovard Field at the University of Southern California. The arrows show where my home runs went. I hit one from each side of the plate in an exhibition game on March 26, 1951. They say that the one that went across the football field went over 600 feet in the air.

This one, on August 6, 1961, was off Pedro Ramos (then with the Minnesota Twins). It was home run #361, and it put me ahead of Joe DiMaggio in All-Time home runs. It was my second home run of the game off Pedro. I also hit another one in the second game of the doubleheader. We won both games. That day I went five for nine, scored five runs, drove in four, and walked three times.

The Pedro Ramos Home Run

This is pitcher Pedro Ramos. Lifetime I hit 12 home runs off Pedro. He was just behind Early Wynn who gave up 13 to me.

One of my favorites was the time I hit the facade off of pitcher Pedro Ramos. We were playing in Washington against the Senators, and one of our pitchers hit some Washington player on purpose. You could tell it was a knock down.

The next inning, I was the lead-off man for the Yankees. I didn't even think anything about it. I just went up to hit, but everybody on our bench and everybody on their bench and even some of the fans knew that Ramos was going to hit me to protect his own players. I didn't blame him. But I hadn't even thought about it.

We were always kind of friendly. I mean, he always wanted to run races with me. And when we would stand around the batting cage before games he used to tease Camilo Pascual, another Washington pitcher, because I had hit a couple of long home runs off of Pascual, and Pascual would tease him about the home runs I had hit off of Ramos. Anyway, he hit me, and I didn't say anything. He didn't try to hit me in the head, he just wanted to hit me because one of their guys got hit.

Well, the next day around the batting cage, he came up to me and said, "Meekie, I'm sorry I had to do that." So I said, "Don't worry about it. But the next time you do it, I'm going to drag a ball down the first base line and run right up your back." He looked at me and said, "You would really do that?"

The funniest thing is that the next time he pitched to me it was in Yankee Stadium, and that's one of the balls I almost hit out of Yankee Stadium. It hit the facade. After the game he told me, "I'd rather have you run up my back than hit one over the roof!"

This is me in the locker room in Detroit after hitting my 400th home run on September 10, 1962. I was the seventh player to do it. It was a solo home run off Tigers' pitcher Hank Aguirre. We won 3-1.

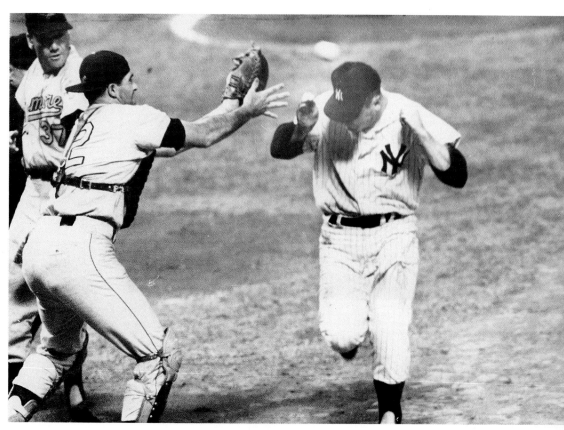

Somebody should have told me to slide here. I scored the winning run in the eighth inning on a single by Tom Tresh. John Orsino is the catcher, and Stu Miller, the pitcher, is backing him up. We won 4-3.

Pitcher Fred Talbot and Tom Tresh (#15) congratulate me after my first home run of the season on April 29, 1967. I hit it off Angels pitcher Jack Sanford. It was career homer #497. We won 4-3.

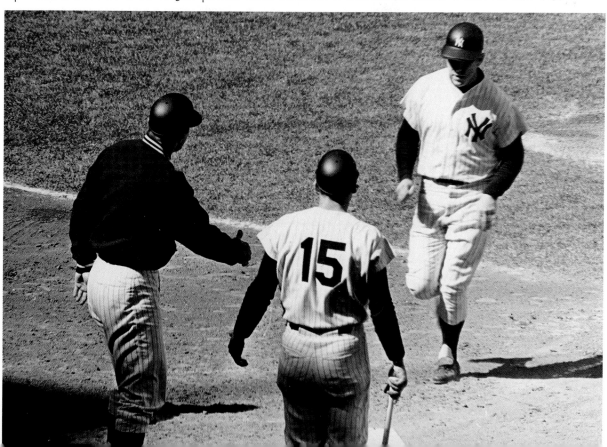

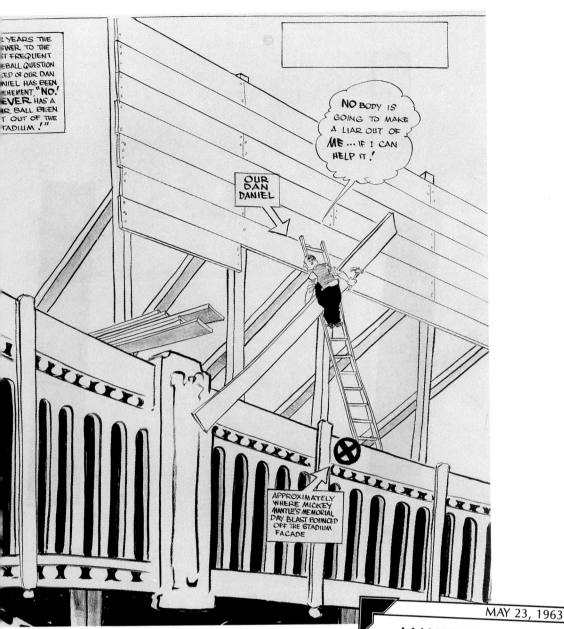

This cartoon came out after I hit the shot off the facade in Yankee Stadium. That was the only home run that I really cared about how far it went. I thought it might go out of the stadium, so I was kind of hoping that it would. No one has ever hit one out of Yankee Stadium.

MAY 23, 1963

MANTLE'S PRODIGIOUS BLAST NEARLY LEAVES STADIUM
Yankees Defeat Athletics in 11th, 8-7
"Hardest Ball I Ever Hit"

NEW YORK— Mickey Mantle left fans breathless with a titanic solo home run in the 11th inning that not only won the game, but almost became the first home run to be hit out of Yankee Stadium. The blast, which was still rising, hit the right field facade only inches from the top and then bounced all the way back to the infield. The clout came off Kansas City pitcher Bill Fischer (6-1).

The dramatic home run came in a most unexpected manner. The Yankees had taken an early 7-0 lead, only to squander it later in the game to force extra innings. Mantle, leading off the 11th, worked the count to 2 balls and 2 strikes before slamming his tremendous drive. Members of both teams thought the ball would leave the stadium. "It was the hardest ball any man ever hit" according to A's coach Jimmy Dykes. Yogi Berra shouted "My God! That's it!" before realizing that the ball might not clear the decorative facade.

In the locker room afterward, Mickey Mantle said "That was the hardest ball I ever hit. I thought it would go out, I really did." Mantle homered off the facade once before, on May 30, 1956 off then Washington Senators pitcher Pedros Ramos.

(see "Yanks Win in 11," page D-2)

The Hardest Ball I Ever Hit

*T*he hardest ball I ever hit was in a night game at Yankee Stadium against Kansas City. Bill Fischer was pitching. It was in the eleventh inning, and it also won the game.

It was a line drive, and I thought it had a chance of making it out of Yankee Stadium. This was the only time I think that I ever really cared how far one of my home runs was going. Usually, as long as it was a home run, that was all I cared about. But this time when I hit it, I thought, "This ball might go out of Yankee Stadium." I was kind of watching it and hoping, but it hit the facade, maybe six inches from the top, and then bounced all the way back to the infield. I think that was probably the hardest ball I ever hit.

Here's a diagram of the hardest ball I ever hit. I hit it in the 11th inning of a game on May 22, 1963, and it won the game. It was off pitcher Bill Fischer of Kansas City. They estimated that it would have gone well over 600 feet if it hadn't hit the facade. What they don't show is that the ball bounced all the way back to the infield. (Photo for illustration purposes only.)

This is Joe Collins. He played first base and the outfield for the Yankees from 1948 through 1957.

Someone asked me one time if I ever went up to bat trying to hit a home run. I told them, "Sure, every time!"

"Go Chase That One!"

Joe Collins, Whitey, and Elston Howard after World Series Game 1 in 1955. Whitey was the winning pitcher, Elston hit a two-run home run, and Joe hit two home runs. Joe's two-run homer in the sixth inning put us ahead to stay.

$\mathcal{E}$arly in my career, I'd been getting some press about hitting long home runs and the guys on the team had been talking. Every once in a while I'd hit one 440 feet or something at Yankee Stadium and everybody would talk about it.

One day we were playing in Cleveland, and I was in the on-deck circle. Joe Collins was hitting second, and he hit a long home run into the upper deck in Municipal Stadium. But he hit it down the line into the upper deck. When I shook hands with Joe as he came by, he said, "Go chase that one, big boy."

Well, that time at bat I did hit one. There used to be a cigarette ad that was a package stuck on the mezzanine in the upper deck in center field. The one I hit went to the left of it, which was probably about 70 feet farther than Joe's ball. When I had rounded the bases and came back into the dugout, everybody was grinning and clapping and pointing at Joe, and Joe was sitting over on the bench with his cap kind of pulled down. I went over to him and said, "What about that one, Joe?" He said, "Aw, go *@#% in your hat!"

This was on September 1, 1963. Me and Whitey went out the night before, because we knew Whitey wouldn't pitch the day after he'd pitched. I'd just gotten off the disabled list, so I didn't think I'd play either. We stayed out pretty late and overslept. We barely made it to the ballpark on time. Sure enough, in the eighth inning, Ralph Houk had me come in to pinch hit. Hank Bauer was coaching for Baltimore then, and he told pitcher Mike McCormick, "Mantle was out late last night, so he's in no condition to hit. Just fire three hard ones across the plate and strike him out." Meanwhile, Whitey pulled me aside and said, "Hey Mick, whatever you do, just swing at the first pitch. He'll probably throw you a strike." Sure enough, he did, and I swung as hard as I could. They say the home run went about 420 feet. It won the game for us, 5-4.

In 1968, Denny McLain had a great year. He won 31 games and lost only six. He's the last pitcher to win at least 30 games in a season.

This is my home run #535 ball, but the funny thing is that Denny McLain is the one who pitched it to me.

*T*he next to the last home run I hit, number 535, broke Jimmy Foxx's record. But the real story behind it is that Denny McLain is the guy that threw it to me.

We were in Detroit and Denny was pitching that day. He was having a great year. I think he won 31 games that year.

The Tigers were about six to nothing ahead of us. It was late in the game, and when I came up to hit, everyone thought that it was going to be my last time up in Detroit. I had already said that I was thinking about retiring. As it turned out, it was my last time up there.

Denny called time out and walked in toward home plate and called Bill Freehan, the catcher, out from behind the plate. He was about five or six feet in front of the plate and he said to Freehan, "Let's let him hit one. This is probably his last time at bat in Detroit."

Well, I heard him, but you never know whether to believe him or not. So when Freehan came back behind the plate, I asked him, "Did I hear what he said, that he wants me to hit a home run?" Freehan said, "Yeah. I mean, he's not going to work on you, he's just going to throw you fast balls." I thought, "Well, great!"

But I was still a little leery, so the first pitch he threw was right down the middle, but I took it. He looked at me as if to say "Hey, what's the matter?" So then, of course, I knew that he really wanted me to hit one. But on the next pitch, I swung a little too hard and I popped it up. It was a foul ball back in the stands. Freehan just got another ball and threw it back out to Denny.

The next pitch he threw me, he really grooved it, and I really hit it good, up into the upper deck. As I was going around first and second, I kind of peeked out at him and he was looking and grinning. When I came around third, I looked right at him and he gave me a great big wink!

Joe Pepitone was the next hitter. He saw what was going on while he was on deck. So when he came up to hit, he looked out at Denny and he said "Hey, right in here, put me one right in here." The first pitch to Pepitone was right behind his head. Denny knocked him down!

Joe Pepitone was always fooling around. In a way he was the first of the modern players. He was the first player I knew who used a hair dryer. Denny McLain wasn't too amused by his antics after home run #535.

"(Denny McLain)'s thinking, 'I laid one in for you, hit it!' He's saying, 'I'll lay one right in for you, hit it!' And sometimes when you know what's comin' it's tough to hit it. They're all grinnin' — Mickey, McLain, and all of 'em, and all of the, uh, rather, the catcher, Freehan, and OH BOY! THERE IT GOES! IT'S A FAIR BALL AND VERY DEEP! Aw, you gotta give that McLain some credit, I wanna tell ya. He's grinning a mile wide. Boy I tell you, you think these ballplayers don't have heart, Frank, and then — THERE'S MICKEY NODDING TO HIM! THANKING HIM! AND BOY, I TELL YOU, I HAVEN'T SEEN ANYTHING LIKE THIS IN MY LIFE! Mantle has now gone ahead of Jimmy Foxx with 535 home runs. And now McLain is — Pepitone says 'Lay one in for me!' and McLain shakes his head at him and says 'No, Sir!'"
— Phil Rizzuto with Frank Messer, actual game call on Yankees Radio, Sept. 19, 1968

Season's Greetings

This was the Yankees'
Christmas Card in 1961. That
was a great year for all of us.

NEW YORK YANKEES
1961 WORLD CHAMPIONS

First Row, Left to Right: WHITEY FORD, BILL SKOWRON, HAL RENIFF, JIM HEGAN, FRANK CROSETTI, RALPH HOUK, JOHN SAIN, WALLY MOSES, EARL TORGESON, CLETIS BOYER, YOGI BERRA, MICKEY MANTLE.
Second Row, Left to Right: GUS MAUCH (TRAINER), BILLY GARDNER, BOB HALE, JOE DE MAESTRI, TONY KUBEK, TEX CLEVENGER, RALPH TERRY, HECTOR LOPEZ, BOB CERV, ELSTON HOWARD, ROGER MARIS, BOB TURLEY, JOE SOARES (TRAINER).
Third Row, Left to Right: BOBBY RICHARDSON, AL DOWNING, LUIS ARROYO, JOHN BLANCHARD, BILL STAFFORD, ROLAND SHELDON, JIM COATES, SPUD MURRAY (BATTING PRACTICE PITCHER), BUD DALEY, BRUCE HENRY (TRAVELING SECRETARY).

Seated on Ground in Front: Batboys FRANK PRUDENTI, FRED BENGIS.

—VI—
1961: The Upside Down Year

Ralph Houk, Roy Haney, and me looking over my $100,000 a year contract. I was the first player to make that amount of money a year.

*T*he best team I ever saw in my life, and I really believe this, was the '61 Yankees. We hit 240 home runs, and I think that Whitey Ford won 25 and lost only four. We had Luis Arroyo in the bullpen and Bill Stafford, Ralph Terry, and Art Ditmar.

Everybody had a great year at the same time. Our infield had Cletis Boyer at third, Tony Kubek at short-stop, Bobby Richardson at second, and Moose Skowron at first. Moose hit 27 home runs that year. Our catchers, Yogi Berra, John Blanchard, and Elston Howard, hit over 60 between the three of them. And of course, me and Roger Maris had phenomenal years.

You know, I never got to see the '27 Yankees. Everybody says that was the greatest team ever. But it would have been a good series, I think, if we'd have had the chance to play them.

When we came out of spring training that year, Ralph Houk, our new manager, had told me that I was the team leader and I mean, I was really up. Like a high school football player, you know, you can get up.

Roger Maris and Louis Arroyo. Roger was "Most Valuable Player" in 1961, and Louis was "Fireman of the Year," or Best Relief Pitcher.

He came out, took me aside and told me that he was going to hit Roger third, and me fourth. He thought that it would help Roger hitting third more than it would help me hitting third in front of everybody. Of course, I'd hit third all my life, but he said, "I'll tell you something: you are our leader, and whatever you do is what we're going to do this year." He started making me feel like I really was the best there was.

I took off like a ball of fire, and I really did kind of carry the club for a while. Roger didn't hit a home run for a long time. I must've been ten or so ahead of him at one time. Anyway, all of a sudden, he got on fire and, like I said, that '61 ballclub was just unbelievable.

Roger, Manager Ralph Houk, and me. 1961 was Ralph's first year managing.

We had some kind of line-up that year. Here's Roger (right field), Yogi Berra (left fielder, catcher), me (center field), Elston Howard (catcher), Moose Skowron (first base), and John Blanchard (catcher, outfielder, utility).

Second baseman Bobby Richardson, pitcher Jim Coates, outfielder Hector Lopez, and third baseman Clete Boyer after we clinched the pennant in 1961. That was just a great team. They say the '27 Yankees were the best team ever, but I think it would've been a great series if we could've played them.

It seemed like everybody wanted us to go on their show back then. This was when we went on "The Match Game."

Bobby Richardson loved kids, and he's done a lot of good work with them. He even went on "Captain Kangaroo" once.

Yogi Berra (second row, third from left) and Joe Garagiola (first row on left) grew up in East St. Louis together. They've been friends all their lives. This was one of their first teams.

Yogi was a great catcher. Here he's blocking the plate and getting the out.

Yogi Berra

Yogi was a great player. He was "Most Valuable Player" three times: 1951, 1954, and 1955.

Joe Garagiola and Tony Kubek. They went on to become the announcers for the "Game of the Week" on NBC.

Yogi was as good a catcher as I ever saw. I'll tell you, he could come from behind the plate on a bunt and almost always throw the guy out. He had a better arm than everybody thought he did. And he could really block the plate.

Yankee Stadium was made for him, with its short porch in right field. He could hit the ball down the right field line better than anybody I ever saw in my life. And he could hit almost anything thrown to him.

Up in Boston one time, they brought in Mickey McDermott, a left handed pitcher, to knock Yogi down. They told him to throw a knockdown pitch at Yogi. Well, the first pitch he threw to Yogi was right at Yogi's head. And Yogi swung at it over his head like he was tomahawking it and hit it right around the right field foul line. It was a fair ball, for a home run! He was unbelievable. He could hit a ball no matter where you threw it.

Most all the stories you hear about Yogi, I think Joe Garagiola made 'em up. Joe made a name for himself by telling Yogi Berra stories. Of course, they grew up together in St. Louis and are great friends. Joe just loves to talk about Yogi.

I have heard Yogi say some funny things. I was standing with him in front of the Gault Ocean Mile during spring training in Fort Lauderdale once and he really looked good. He had on a Hawaiian flowered shirt, a pair of slacks, and a pair of those tong slippers that they wear down in Florida, without any socks. A little old lady came up to him and said, "Yogi, you look cool today!" And Yogi said, "You don't look too hot yourself!"

One time somebody hollered, "Hey, Yog, what time is it?" He looked at his watch and said, "Oh, you mean right now?"

Everybody always thinks of Yogi as a catcher. What most people don't realize is that in 1961 Yogi was our left fielder. He played the most games of any left fielder. He caught some, too.

Yogi on the "Ed Sullivan Show." A lot of us were invited to go on Sullivan's show over the years.

Yogi went on to manage the Yankees a couple of times. We won the American League pennant under Yogi in 1964.

Yogi catching a foul pop-up. Yogi knew Yankee Stadium so well that, if a foul ball was hit behind him, he could tell where it was going, and he wouldn't even chase it if it was going to be out of reach. He could tell when it was going to be too far back in the stands.

Yogi and his son, Timmy. Yogi has three sons, Larry, Dale, and Timmy.

"Boy, You Stunk!"

I remember I'd had one of my worst days that I'd ever had, I guess. I'd struck out two or three times with men in scoring position and I dropped a pop fly that cost us the game. Bob Turley was the pitcher. I never will forget that. Of course, he was a nice guy. He came over after the game and said, "Forget it, Mick." I really felt bad. I didn't mind striking out. I was getting used to that by then, but to drop a pop fly and let the winning run in was really bad.

Anyway, I went right straight to my locker and threw my glove and my cap down. I was sitting on my stool in front of my locker with my head in my hands. It was so bad, that the reporters didn't even come in. They knew I was gonna be pretty hot.

As I was just sitting there holding my head, I could feel somebody looking at me. I looked up out from under my hands and there was this little kid standing there. It was Yogi's son, Timmy. Yogi's locker was right next to mine. I looked at him and I said, "Hey, Timmy, how're you doing?" Then I said, "What's the matter?"

He was looking at me really funny. Then he looked me right in the eye and he said, "Boy, you stunk!" Yogi jumped out of his locker and gave him a boot in the butt. He kicked him about four feet out of there and went over and got him and shook him and took him into the player's lounge where he couldn't say anything else!

Roger Maris. A great ballplayer. He was "Most Valuable Player" in 1960 and 1961.

Roger Maris

In 1961, when Roger broke Babe Ruth's single season home run record, I hit 54 home runs. I won home run titles four times. That year I hit the most I ever hit in a season, but I didn't win the title, Roger did.

P robably one of the questions I get more than anything else is, "What about Roger Maris and yourself?" In 1961, when Roger hit the 61 home runs, there was a lot written that we didn't like each other, that we argued a lot, or fought a lot, or something. That's the farthest thing from the truth. In fact, we lived together on the road. Roger was one of my closest friends, and we used to just joke about all of the headlines that said we were fighting and arguing and mad at each other.

When you think about Roger Maris, the first thing you think about is home runs. I think it's the single hardest thing to do in sports. And to hit 61 of them is *really* hard. But outside of the home runs, the fact that he hit 61 home runs in a single season and nobody else ever has, makes Roger one of the greatest players I've ever seen. I mean, he was as good a fielder as I've ever seen. He had a great arm. He never made a mistake, like throwing a ball too high and letting a guy take an extra base. He was a great base runner. I never saw him make a mistake on the bases. He was always in the game. He was also a good team man. All the guys really liked him, and everyone was really pulling for him at the end.

Roger was a great player. He was a "Gold Glove" outfielder, and he had a great arm. Here he's backing me up on the play, showing me where to throw the ball, just like you're supposed to do.

MARIS' HOME RUN RECORD LOSES ASTERISK

Roger with Roger, Jr. and the "Hickok Belt" for Athlete of the Year.

Roger was invited to the White House, where he met President Kennedy.

Here's Roger receiving his "Gold Glove Award" for the 1960 season.

Roger loved to eat crab, and Maryland is famous for its crab. When we were in Baltimore we'd buy crabs and beer, fill our bathtub with ice and have a party in our room. We had some great times in Baltimore. This is a picture of a home run I hit in Baltimore on August 10, 1957 off pitcher Ray Moore. They said it was the first ball to clear the hedge behind the fence in center field. I went four for five in that game, scored two runs, drove in three runs, and stole a base. We won that game 6-3.

The Roger Maris Swimming Pool Race

It seems like I'm always signing autographs. Most of the time I don't mind doing it, though.

We had an off day in Baltimore and Bob Turley lived in Baltimore. He invited everybody over to his house for a little cookout. We had steak and some beer and stuff, and we were all having a pretty good time.

I used to say, no matter what people were talking about, that I was the Oklahoma State Champion at it. No matter what somebody said. Well, we were sitting around talking by the pool and Roger was telling me about his swimming.

He really was an all-around athlete. He was a great football player in Fargo, North Dakota. And baseball and basketball, and I guess he was a great swimmer. Heck, I can't even swim. But I told him I was the Oklahoma State Champion and I'd like to race him across Turley's pool.

Well, I got Whitey off to the side, and I said, "Hey, Slick, when we dive in the water, get that pool sweep over there, and stick it in the water. I'll grab a hold of it and you run me down to the other end." So he said okay.

Me and Roger got out there in this stance, just like they do in the Olympics, a diving stance. Just as soon as I dived in, Whitey handed me the pole, and ran me down to the other end. But he didn't run straight. He ran kind of sideways, and I was bouncing off of the side of the pool.

Anyway, he got me down there a good ten feet ahead of Roger and I jumped up on the edge of the pool. I was sitting there when Roger got there. I was wiping the water off of my face, shaking my hair and he looks up and he says, "How in the hell did you get here?" He knew he could beat me. He didn't have any idea what happened. Then everybody started laughing and giggling about it.

Pretty soon, he noticed that the whole left side of my arm was almost bleeding from Whitey pulling me against the side. He said, "You son of a gun!" He knew then that I didn't really swim down there.

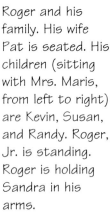

Roger and his family. His wife Pat is seated. His children (sitting with Mrs. Maris, from left to right) are Kevin, Susan, and Randy. Roger, Jr. is standing. Roger is holding Sandra in his arms.

Me and my family sitting by the pool. (From left to right) There's Danny, Mickey Jr., Billy, David, and my wife, Merlyn.

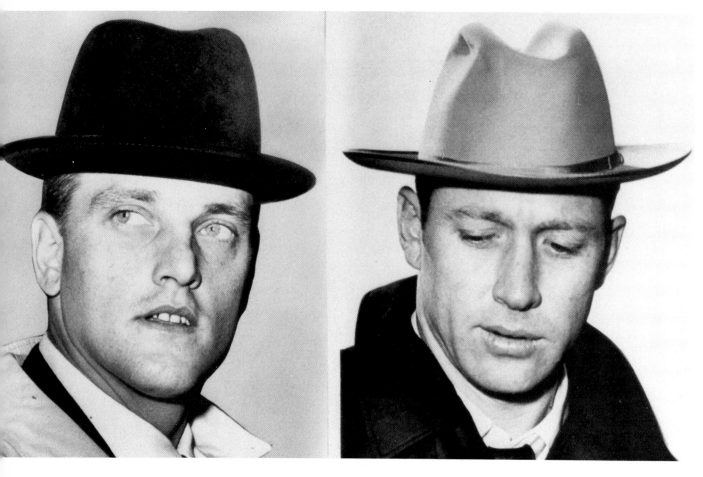

Roger and me. Take a look at those hats.

In 1960, I hit 40 home runs and Roger hit 39. They added up to 79, so they had us hold up our jersey numbers to signify the total.

The M & M Boys

Roger congratulates me after a home run.

I can remember that year, once it got far enough into the season, it looked like both me and Roger had a chance of breaking Babe Ruth's record. They called us the "M & M Boys." Almost every newspaper the day after a game would have the M & M Boys in the headline. I don't care if Kubek, Richardson, Cletis Boyer, Moose, Elston, Yogi, or anyone, had hit a home run that won the game, it would still say what the M & M Boys did in the headlines.

The players were so good about it. They made it easy on us, because they would tease us instead of getting mad about it. They didn't say, "Hey, look, I hit a home run and they put the M & M Boys in the headline." They would come around and say, "Hey, what did the M & M Boys do today?" They teased us a lot and they took it really good. They made it a lot easier, especially for Roger after I fell out of the race. I mean, they helped him do it. The whole team did.

In 1961 Roger and I became so popular that we got lots of offers after the season for all sorts of things. One was for a movie, mainly for kids, called, "Safe at Home." It was about a little kid who told all of his friends that he knew me and Roger and he ended up sneaking into spring training camp to meet us. I remember that one of my lines in the movie was, "That would be like calling a foul ball fair," where I was trying to explain to the kid that by fibbing about being friends with us he had done the wrong thing. I don't know why, but I had all kinds of trouble with that line. For some reason I just couldn't get it right, and it took something like 20 takes for me to finally get it.

We got a lot of visitors that year from some really famous people. This is me and Roger with Doris Day.

In 1961, Roger and me combined for 115 home runs. He hit 61 and I hit 54. I don't think any two players will ever hit that many again. After I hit #48, I told Roger, "Well, I beat my guy. Now it's up to you to catch yours." I was talking about Lou Gehrig, who hit 47 in 1927. Babe Ruth hit 60 in 1927.

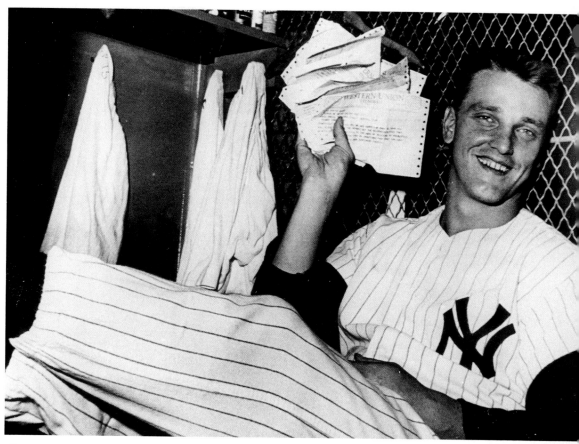

Roger got a lot of mail that year. Some of it was pretty mean, which I never really understood. Here he's holding telegrams congratulating him for breaking Babe Ruth's record.

Roger, Mrs. Babe Ruth, and me at Yankee Stadium. She came to a lot of the games that year.

M&M: MANTLE HITS 3 HRs, NOW HAS 43
Yankees Sweep Marathon Twinbill, 7-6 & 3-2

AUG. 7, 1961, NEW YORK— Mickey Mantle continued his torrid pace in quest of Babe Ruth's single season home run record yesterday by homering three times in the Yankees doubleheader against the Minnesota Twins. All three home runs were hit left handed.

Mantle homered twice in the first game off pitcher Pedro Ramos, allowing the Yankees to keep pace and pull out a win in the 15th inning. Mantle's second homer was his 361st, putting him ahead of Joe DiMaggio on the all-time home run list.

After homering is his first two at bats, Mantle doubled in the tying run in the fifth inning to make the score 5-5. The Twins scored the go ahead run in the top of the 10th, only to be tied agin in the bottom of the 10th by John Blanchard's solo home run. In the 15th inning, with runners on 2nd and 3rd, Mantle was intentionally walked to load the bases. Yogi Berra drove in the winning (see "Yankees" page C-3)

August 12, 1961

Mickey Clouts #44, Roger #42
Yanks Bomb Nats 12-5

Roger and me heading out to the field. Roger was my roommate on the road. We had a lot of fun together. I'll tell you, I was really pulling for him to break the record at the end of '61. The whole team was.

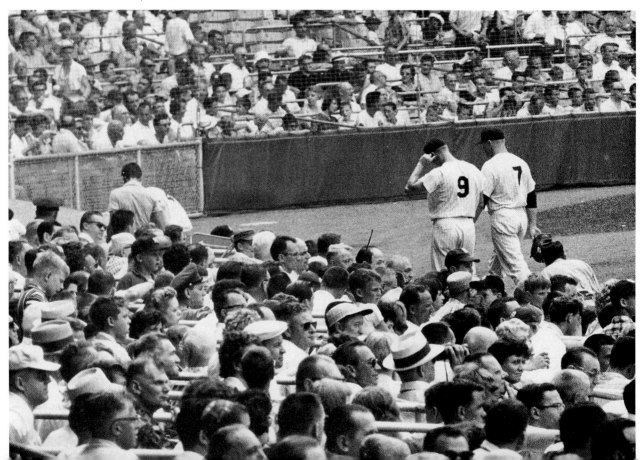

The Home Run Race

Roger in the locker room after he hit his 61st home run. He hit it on the last day of the season off pitcher Tracy Stallard of the Boston Red Sox. They made a big deal out of the 162-game schedule, but nobody's even come close to his record since he set it.

*Y*ou know, I didn't get to finish the season that year. I had a real bad cold. We were in Boston and one of the announcers told me on the way back home to New York, "You know Mick, those antibiotics that you're taking aren't doing you any good." He said, "I know a doctor that you might be able to go to that can give you a shot that can get rid of that cold. Then you'll feel better and be able to play better."

So I said, "Well, I'll try anything, because I want to stay in the race." I was only two or three home runs behind Roger at that time. Anyway, I went to this doctor and I got a shot in the hip and it turned bad. I got up the next morning and I had a 104 degree temperature. I had to go to the hospital and have it lanced. So I spent the last week and a half of the season watching from my hospital bed.

That made the pressure twice as bad on Roger, because there was only one guy that the reporters could come to. For Roger to have gone ahead and broken the record, I think was just unbelievable. I think it was the greatest thing I've ever seen in sports. I was so proud of him.

And the way he acted. He never ran around the bases jumping up and down, or hit a home run and stood at home plate and watched it go out like they do nowadays. When he hit a home run, he ran around the bases just like he always did. He was a real class act. I even cried when he hit his 61st home run.

"We've only got a handful of people sitting out in left field, but in right field, man, it's hogged out there! And they're standing up! Here's the windup. Fastball. HIT DEEP TO RIGHT! THIS COULD BE IT! WAY BACK THERE. HOLY COW, HE DID IT! 61 FOR MARIS! Look at 'em go for that ball out there. HOLY COW! WHAT A SHOT! Another standing ovation for Roger Maris, and they want him to come out and take a bow. He does. MAN, DO YOU SEE THIS?! HE WANTS TO SIT DOWN AND THEY WON'T LET HIM!"
— Phil Rizzuto, actual game call on Yankees Radio, Oct. 1, 1961

This one tells you a lot about Roger. After he hit his 61st home run, the crowd wanted him to come out for a bow. He didn't want to do it, he was so modest. So the players had to push him out. If you look, you can see one of the guys pushing him.

The Home Run Record

This is the baseball Roger gave me.

When Roger hit his 61st home run, he came into the dugout and they were all applauding. I mean, this is something that's only happened once in baseball, right? And the people were all applauding. They wanted him to come back out. He wouldn't come out, so the players had to push him back out. They forced him to come out and take a bow. That's the kind of guy he was. He was great, and I really liked him.

I think it was stupid to have an asterisk behind his home run record, and I'm glad they finally removed it. There have been a lot of guys who have tried since then, and nobody's ever even come close.

I don't know why he hasn't been selected for the Hall of Fame. To me, he's as good as there ever was. I have four boys of my own, and if I could pick somebody for those boys to grow up to be like, it would be Roger.

Out of all the trophies that I have, I think the one thing that I treasure more than anything else is a ball that Roger gave me. It's got his picture on it, and he wrote on it: "To Mickey, the greatest of them all. Best always, Roger Maris."

Sam Gordon, a restaurant owner in Sacramento, had offered $5,000 for the 61st home run ball. When Sal Durante tried to give the ball to Roger, Roger told Sal he should take the money. Sam gave the ball to Roger, who gave it to the Hall of Fame. That's the kind of guy Roger was. Sal used the money to get married. Here's Roger, Sam Gordon, and Sal.

This was after I broke my foot when my spikes caught in the fence in Baltimore in 1963. I did have a lot of injuries. For example, I missed several games at the end of the home run race. That made the pressure twice as bad on Roger. The fact that he went ahead and broke the record is the greatest thing I've ever seen in sports.

Here's another shot of Roger with President Kennedy in the White House.

Norm Cash ("Batting Title"), Roger ("Sultan of Swat Award"), and Whitey ("Cy Young Award").

MARIS HITS #61!

Ruth's Single-Season Record Broken!
Commissioner Frick May Attach Asterisk to Mark

OCT. 2, 1961, NEW YORK— Roger Maris set the single-season home run record when he hit his 61st home run, besting Babe Ruth's previous total of 60 in 1927. Maris' blast came off right-hand pitcher Tracy Stallard of the Boston Red Sox in the fourth inning of the Yankees 163rd game.

Maris' home run brings to a head the controversy raging around this year's change from the previous 154-game schedule to the new 162-game schedule. Baseball Commissioner Ford Frick has stated that he is in favor of placing a "distinguishing mark" in record books denoting that Maris' accomplishment took place under the new expanded scheduling.

"It must be taken into account. (See "Maris Sets Record," page 3)

American League President Joe Cronin presents Roger with the Most Valuable Player Award for 1961.

Sunday, March 2, 1969

MANTLE RETIRES FROM BASEBALL AFTER 18 YEARS

Hanging up #7 for the last time. That was one of the saddest days of my life.

MICKEY MANTLE RETIRES FROM BASEBALL!

Baseball Loses a Legendary Player

MARCH 2, 1969—NEW YORK— Baseball legend Mickey Mantle announced his retirement from the game in a tearful press conference. Mantle, who has played 18 seasons for the New York Yankees, said that he was leaving the game because his skills had eroded and "There's just no use trying anymore."

Plagued by injuries throughout his career, the Yankee slugger has become a household name because of his tremendous home runs. His lifetime total of 536 home runs puts him third on the all-time home run list. Mantle has arguably hit some of the longest home runs in baseball history, including a 565-foot drive out of the old Griffith Stadium in Washington, D.C. and two home runs that hit the facade at Yankee Stadium, almost leaving the park. His list of prodigious home runs in every ballpark is seemingly endless.

His list of accomplishments and records is impressive. A three-time Most Valuable Player, he led the league in home runs four times. He played in 12 World Series and won seven. He holds the record for the most World Series home runs with 18. His 2,401 games is a New York Yankees record (see "Career Summary" page D-5).

Mantle, a native Oklahoman, was signed by the Yankees in 1949, fresh out of high school. He joined the team in 1951 after an impressive spring training during which he hit .402 with (see "Mantle Retires" page D-5)

— VII —
Reflections

From the press conference announcing his retirement:

" *...And I don't hit the ball when I need to, and I can't steal second when I need to. I can't go from first to third or score from second on base hits. And I just think it's time that I quit tryin'."*

The press conference where I announced my retirement from baseball on March 1, 1969.

On the first "Mickey Mantle Day" at Yankee Stadium on September 9, 1965 they gave me two quarter horses.

Mayor Wagner proclaimed September 18, 1969 as "Mickey Mantle Day" in New York City.

I was the first to receive the "Hutch Award," named after Fred Hutchinson. The Baseball Writers of America gave it to me in 1965. Hutch, who had managed the Tigers, the Cardinals, and the Reds, had died of cancer the year before. Everyone really liked him.

They gave me the "Hickok Belt" for Professional Athlete of the Year in 1956 when I won the Triple Crown.

Here I am receiving my third "Most Valuable Player Award" for 1962 from American League President Joe Cronin.

Cardinal Spellman gave me this award for some charity work I had done. This was in 1957.

The "Sid Mercer Memorial Award" was given to me on February 13, 1957 by the New York Baseball Writers Association. Sid was the baseball writer the award was named after.

SUNDAY, JANUARY 20, 1957

MANTLE IS VOTED PLAYER OF THE YEAR

Yankee to Get Mercer Award at Baseball Dinner Feb. 3

The Philadelphia Sports Writers Association gave me "The Most Courageous Athlete Award" for the 1962 season. You can read the names of some of the other athletes who got it before me.

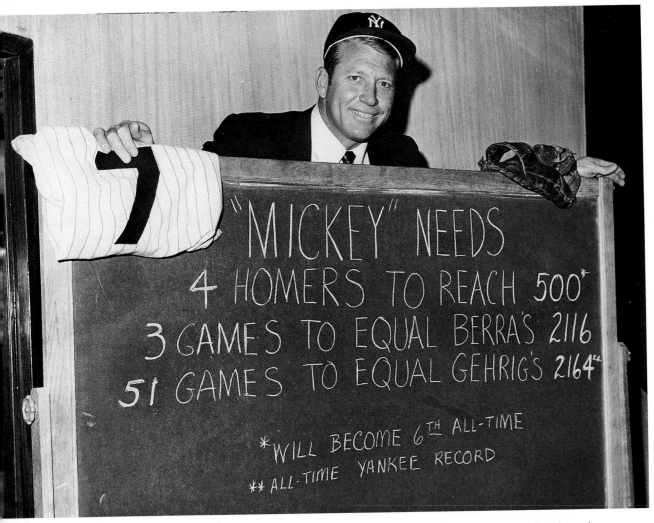

This was at the beginning of the 1967 season. They made up a blackboard with a list of accomplishments I was nearing.

Me and my family, around 1960. That's my wife Merlyn holding Danny, then Billy, me, David, and Mickey Jr.

This portrait of me and my family was given to me before an exhibition game we played against the Mets in 1968. Gil Hodges, the great Dodgers player, is standing next to me. That was his first year as manager of the Mets.

"Mickey Mantle Day," June 8, 1969. Yankee Stadium was packed with almost 70,000 people. It won't even hold that many anymore.

Mickey Mantle Day

I think the biggest thrill I've ever had was in 1969. They declared Mickey Mantle Day at Yankee Stadium. Something like 69,000 or 71,000 people showed up. I don't think the Stadium will even hold that many now.

(From Mickey Mantle Day at Yankee Stadium) *Mel Allen: "A magnificent Yankee, the great number seven, Mickey Mantle!"*

Mickey Mantle: "When I walked into this stadium 18 years ago, I felt much the same way I do right now. I don't have words to describe how I felt then or how I feel now, but I'll tell you one thing, baseball was real good to me and playing 18 years in Yankee Stadium is the best thing that could ever happen to a ballplayer."

My wife Merlyn and me at the first "Mickey Mantle Day" in 1965.

At that time they had only retired numbers three, four and five. For Ruth, Gehrig, and DiMaggio. And for a kid from Oklahoma to have his number retired with those three guys is the biggest thrill you could ever have.

I remember that they drove me around Yankee Stadium that day on a golf cart. And the guy that I was driving around with was Danny, one of the ground crew guys who came up at about the same time I did in '51. I'd known him all my life.

As we got to center field or a little past center field, I told him, "Danny, do you know what? This makes me feel like Dolly Parton's little baby when it's nursing. Is this all for me?"

A whole group of kids brought posters on "Mickey Mantle Day" and
paraded them around the field. It was really something.

Bobby Kennedy came to the first "Mickey Mantle Day" in 1965.

Here I'm wiping tears from my eyes on "Mickey Mantle Day" on June 8, 1969. That day was one of my greatest thrills.

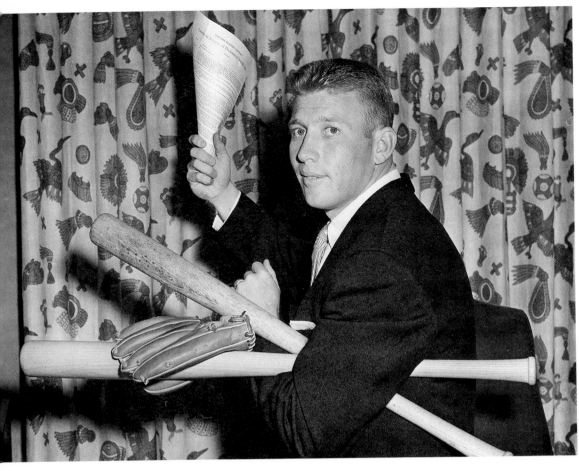

Here I am holding one of my contracts. People always ask me what I think I'd make if I were playing now.

Here I am in the locker room after a game. The press used to gather around my locker, particularly if I'd had a good game. It got really crowded sometimes. I tried to answer their questions. I mean, they were only doing their jobs.

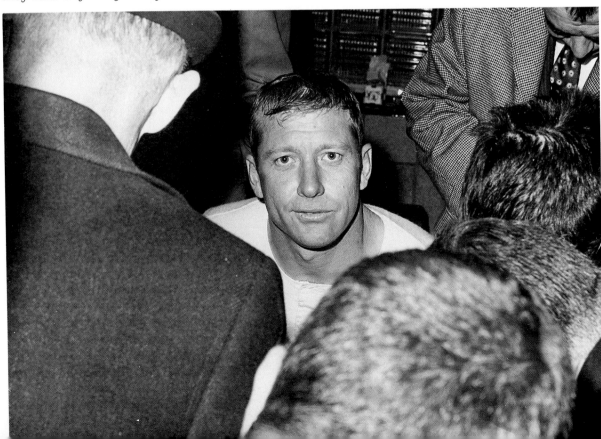

If I Were Playing Now

Everybody says to me, "Mick, how much do you think you would make now if you were still playing?" I like what Joe DiMaggio said. He said he'd go up and knock on the door at Yankee Stadium. When George Steinbrenner opened the door he'd say, "Hi, pardner." I've always liked that.

This is me with Teresa Brewer, the singer. She had just recorded a song called, "I Like Mickey." I was in the song, too. One of my two big lines was to say, "Mickey who?" after she sang, "I like Mickey." It wasn't exactly a big hit record.

They held a press conference to announce my contract signing in 1962. You can see manager Ralph Houk to right of me and Howard Cosell sitting next to Ralph. Of course, Howard became famous when he went on "Monday Night Football" years later.

Sometimes it seems like I'm always
signing autographs. I'm not complaining,
but I really don't understand it.

Signing an autograph for Lee Remick and
her son after a game. A lot of celebrities
came by to visit with us and get
autographs.

One More Autograph

Well, I don't know for what reason, but for some reason or other I seem to be more popular now than I've ever been in my life. I don't know if it's the bubble gum card craze or what. But autograph seekers just seem to come from everywhere.

I know that my bubble gum card sells for thousands of dollars now. Nothing seems to stop 'em, you know.

Not too long ago, I remember they thought I was having a heart attack on an airplane. I had a real bad cold. It was almost like walking pneumonia or something — I could hardly breathe on the plane. I was getting a little scared myself, so I asked the stewardess, "What do you do if somebody has a heart attack?" She looked at me and she said, "My God, you better go sit down. I'll give you some oxygen."

They called the paramedics and they came to the door of the plane when it arrived in Dallas. I still had the oxygen on me that they had put on in the plane. They put me on a stretcher and put the thing in my nose and the oxygen on my face. They were pulling me out of there and some guy was standing outside the door. He yells "Hey, that's Mickey Mantle!" And he says, "Say Mick, would you sign this for me?" He had a piece of paper and pen for me to sign.

Well, they went ahead and took me to the hospital and checked me all over. The next day they gave me an angiogram (a heart test), to see how my heart was. It turned out I was okay, and I just had a very bad cold.

But I got to thinking about that guy wanting an autograph. I mean, as far as he knew, I was dying. I went to New York pretty soon after that, so I made up a story for the New York press.

I told them that I'd dreamed that night that I'd died and gone to heaven. I finally got in to see God and God said, "Well, Mick, I'm sorry, but we can't keep you up here because of the way you acted on Earth." But he said, "Would you do me a favor?" I said, "What's that, God?" He said "Before you go, would you sign those two dozen baseballs there for me?" And I thought that was really funny.

I've signed a lot of autographs for charity. Here I'm signing for St. Vincent's Hospital.

Here I'm signing autographs for some of the kids back in Oklahoma.

I think a lot of kids kind of felt about me the way I'd felt about Stan Musial when I was a kid. I never forgot that, so I always tried to make some time for them.

Posing with a Junior Fire Marshal during spring training in St. Petersburg in 1958.

The Mick's Message to Kids

Well, that's about it for now. I'd just like to finish up by saying to all you kids out there:

Stay away from drugs and alcohol. Go to school and listen to your teachers. And most of all listen to your moms and dads. You can be anything you want to be in this country of ours, and as good as you set your mind to be. Guys like Stan Musial, Willie Mays, Hank Aaron, all the guys that took care of themselves are up at the top in the stats of life now, not only in baseball. So be sure and take good care of yourselves and go out there and do it. Make us all proud of you.

I did a lot of different things for charity. Here I acted as referee for the Miss Teenage America Turtle Derby one year.

Here I am visiting in the Yankees dugout after I retired, which was one of the few moments I've had to relax. Nowadays it seems as if I'm busier than I ever was. People seem to recognize me everywhere I go. Sometimes they don't though. Once I was flying on a commercial jet flight, and we got into some bad weather. This was when the Yankees weren't doing too good, I think they were in last place or something. The pilot was a fan, so he took a break and came back to first class to meet me and talk to me. After a few minutes, the plane really began to jump around, so he got up to back to the cabin. As he left he said to me, "Boy Mick, we could sure use you today." You know, about playing with the Yankees. I guess the guy next to me didn't who I was because he looked at me and asked, "Are you a pilot, too?"

— VIII —
Appendix

Lifetime Record

Year	Club	League	Pos.	G.	AB.	R.	H.	2B	3B	HR.	RBI.	B.A.	PO.	A.	E.	F.A
1949	Independence	K-O-M	SS	89	323	54	101	15	7	7	63	.313	121	245	47	.886
1950	Joplin	W.A.	SS	137	519	*141	*199	30	12	26	136	*.383	202	340	55	.908
1951	New York	Amer.	OF	96	341	61	91	11	5	13	65	.267	135	4	6	.959
1951	Kansas City	A.A.	OF	40	166	32	60	9	3	11	50	.361	110	4	4	.966
1952	New York	Amer.	OF-3B	142	549	94	171	37	7	23	87	.311	348	16	*14	.963
1953	New York	Amer.	OF-SS	127	461	105	136	24	3	21	92	.295	322	10	6	.982
1954	New York	Amer.	OF-1F	146	543	*129	163	17	12	27	102	.300	344	*25	9	.976
1955	New York	Amer.	OF-SS	147	517	121	158	25	11	*37	99	.306	376	11	2	.995
1956	New York	Amer.	OF	150	533	*132	188	22	5	*52	*130	*.353	370	10	4	.990
1957	New York	Amer.	OF	144	474	*121	173	28	6	34	94	.365	324	6	7	.979
1958	New York	Amer.	OF	150	519	*127	158	21	1	*42	97	.304	331	5	8	.977
1959	New York	Amer.	OF	144	541	104	154	23	4	31	75	.285	366	7	2	*.995
1960	New York	Amer.	OF	153	527	*119	145	17	6	*40	94	.275	326	9	3	.991
1961	New York	Amer.	OF	153	514	132	163	16	6	54	128	.317	351	6	6	.983
1962	New York	Amer.	OF	123	377	96	121	15	1	30	89	.321	214	4	5	.978
1963	New York	Amer.	OF	65	172	40	54	8	0	15	35	.314	99	2	1	.990
1964	New York	Amer.	OF	143	465	92	141	25	2	35	111	.303	217	3	5	.978
1965	New York	Amer.	OF	122	361	44	92	12	1	19	46	.255	165	3	6	.966
1966	New York	Amer.	OF	108	333	40	96	12	1	23	56	.288	172	2	0	1.000
1967	New York	Amer.	1B	144	440	63	108	17	0	22	55	.245	1089	91	8	.993
1968	New York	Amer.	1B	144	435	57	103	14	1	18	54	.237	1195	76	15	.988
Major League Totals				2,401	8,102	1,677	2,415	344	72	536	1,509	.298	6,734	290	107	.984

*Denotes led league

World Series Record

Year	Club	League	Pos.	G.	AB.	R.	H.	2B	3B	HR.	RBI.	B.A.	PO.	A.	E.	F.A
1951	New York	Amer.	OF	2	5	1	1	0	0	0	0	.200	4	0	0	1.000
1952	New York	Amer.	OF	7	29	5	10	1	1	2	3	.345	16	0	0	1.000
1953	New York	Amer.	OF	6	24	3	5	0	0	2	7	.208	14	0	0	1.000
1955	New York	Amer.	OF-PH	3	10	1	2	0	0	1	1	.200	4	0	0	1.000
1956	New York	Amer.	OF	7	24	6	6	1	0	3	4	.250	18	1	0	1.000
1957	New York	Amer.	OF-PH	6	19	3	5	0	0	1	2	.263	8	0	1	1.000
1958	New York	Amer.	OF	7	24	4	6	0	1	2	3	.250	16	0	1	.889
1960	New York	Amer.	OF	7	25	8	10	1	0	3	11	.400	15	0	0	1.000
1961	New York	Amer.	OF	2	6	0	1	0	0	0	0	.167	2	0	0	1.000
1962	New York	Amer.	OF	7	25	2	3	1	0	0	0	.120	11	0	0	1.000
1963	New York	Amer.	OF	4	15	1	2	0	0	1	1	.133	6	0	0	1.000
1964	New York	Amer.	OF	7	24	8	8	2	0	3	8	.333	12	0	2	.857
World Series Totals				65	230	42	59	6	2	18	40	.257	126	1	3	.977

All Star Game Record

Year	League	Pos.	AB.	R.	H.	2B	3B	HR.	RBI.	B.A.	PO.	A.	E.	F.A
1953	American	OF	2	0	0	0	0	0	0	.000	0	0	0	.000
1954	American	OF	5	1	2	0	0	0	0	.400	2	0	0	1.000
1955	American	OF	6	1	2	0	0	1	3	.333	3	0	0	1.000
1956	American	OF	4	1	1	0	0	1	1	.250	0	0	0	.000
1957	American	OF	4	1	1	0	0	0	0	.250	4	0	0	1.000
1958	American	OF	2	0	1	0	0	0	0	.500	3	0	0	1.000
1959	American (both games)	OF	3	0	1	0	0	0	0	.333	3	0	0	1.000
1960	American (both games)	OF	4	0	1	0	0	0	0	.250	5	0	0	1.000
1961	American (both games)	OF	6	0	0	0	0	0	0	.000	5	0	0	1.000
1962	American (first game)	OF	1	0	0	0	0	0	0	.000	0	0	0	1.000
1964	American	OF	4	1	1	0	0	0	0	.250	2	0	0	1.000
1967	American	PH	1	0	0	0	0	0	0	.000	0	0	0	.000
All-Star Game Totals			42	5	10	0	0	2	4	.238	27	0	0	1.000

Records, Awards, and Achievements (Partial List)

RECORDS *(When He Retired)*:

3rd Highest Career Home Run Total — *536*

Most Games as a Yankee — *2,401*

Most World Series Home Runs — *18*

Most World Series RBIs — *40*

Most World Series Runs — *42*

Most World Series Walks — *43*

Most Home Runs by Position, Career — *OF 496*

Most Home Runs by a Switch Hitter — *536*

Most Games with Switch Hit Home Runs in One Game — *10 (Total 21 HRs)*

Most Extra-Inning Home Runs, Career — *14*

Most Pitch Hit-Hit Home Runs, Career — *7*

Most Home Runs in Final Season — *1968: G 144; AB 435; HR 18*

Most Two Home Run Games — *46*

Longest Measured Home Run in Regular Season Major League Game (565 ft.) — *Griffith Stadium, Washington; April 17, 1953*

Home Runs in Most Consecutive At-Bats, AL (4) — *July 4, 1962 - 2; July 6, 1962 - 2*

Best Home Run Ratio, Career — *HR 536; AB 8102; Ratio 15.12*

Participating Player, Most Players (2) on a Team with 50 or More Home Runs (Single Season), AL — *NY Yankees, 1961: Roger Maris, 61; Mickey Mantle, 54*

Participating Player, Most Players (2) on a Team with 40 or More Home Runs (Single Season), AL — *NY Yankees, 1961: Roger Maris, 61; Mickey Mantle, 54*

Participating Player, Most Players (6) on a Team with 20 or More Home Runs (Single Season), AL — *NY Yankees, 1961: Roger Maris, 61; Mickey Mantle, 54; Bill Skowron, 28; Yogi Berra, 22; Elston Howard, 21; Johnny Blanchard, 21*

Participating Player, Team with Most Home Runs in a Game (7), AL — *NY Yankees, May 30, 1961: Mickey Mantle, 2; Roger Maris, 2; Bill Skowron, 2; Yogi Berra, 1*

Participating Player, Best Home Run Trio, Season, AL — *NY Yankees, 1961: Roger Maris, 61; Mickey Mantle, 54; Bill Skowron, 28; Total 153*

Participating Player, Best Home Run Duo, Season, AL — *NY Yankees, 1961: Roger Maris, 61; Mickey Mantle, 54; Total 115*

Participating Player, Team with Most Home Runs in a Single Season, AL — *NY Yankees, 1961: Total 240*

AWARDS

Most Valuable Player — *1956, 1957, 1962*

AL Home Run Champion — *1955 (37), 1956 (52), 1958 (42), 1960 (40)*

AL Batting Champion — *1956 (.353)*

AL RBI Champion — *1956 (130)*

AL Slugging Champion — *1956 (.705), 1961 (.687)*

AL Runs Scored Champion — *1954 (129), 1956 (132), 1957 (121), 1958 (127), 1960 (119), 1961 (132)*

Triple Crown Winner — *1956 (52 HRs; .353 Avg.; 130 RBIs) (Led both leagues in each category)*

Hickok Belt Award Winner (Professional Athlete of the Year) - *1956*

Sultan of Swat Award Winner — *1956*

Sid Mercer Memorial Award Winner (Player of the Year) — *1957*

Hutch Award Winner (Baseball Writers of America) — *1965*

Mickey Mantle Day Proclamation, City of New York — *September 18, 1969*

Most Courageous Athlete Award (Philadelphia Sports Writers) — *1962*

Mickey Mantle Day, Yankee Stadium, New York — *September 9, 1965*

Mickey Mantle Day, Yankee Stadium, New York — *June 8, 1969*

Mickey Mantle Day, Commerce, Oklahoma — *1952*

Griggs Trophy (Oklahoma Athlete of the Year) — *1952*

Member, AL Champions — *1951, 1952, 1953, 1955, 1956, 1957, 1958, 1960, 1961, 1962, 1963, 1964*

Member, World Champions — *1951, 1952, 1953, 1956, 1958, 1961, 1962*

Number Retired, NY Yankees, AL — *#7, June 8, 1969*

Elected to Hall of Fame in First Year of Eligibility — *January 16, 1974*

Inducted into Hall of Fame — *August 12, 1974*

ACHIEVEMENTS

Grand Slam Home Runs, AL (9) — *July 26, 1952; July 29, 1952; July 6, 1953; May 18, 1955; July 30, 1956; May 2, 1961; August 19, 1962; June 18, 1965; July 23, 1966*

World Series Grand Slam Home Runs (1) — *October 6, 1952*

Inside the Park Home Runs (6) — *August 7, 1953; May 9, 1958; May 20, 1958; June 5, 1958; May 12, 1959; June 30, 1961*

Home Runs in Both Games of Doubleheader (11) — *June 19, 1951; July 13, 1952; July 26, 1953; July 10, 1955; May 30, 1956; July 1, 1958; August 16, 1959; August 6, 1961; May 6, 1962; May 6, 1964; July 8, 1966 (Total 25 HRs)*

Back-to-Back Home Runs (With other players) — *39 times*

Pinch Hit Grand Slams, AL (1) — *July 6, 1953, Opponent: Philadelphia Athletics, Pitcher: Frank Fanovich*

Three Home Runs in One Game, AL — *May 13, 1955*

Participating Player, Three Consecutive Home Runs, AL — *June 29, 1966; 3rd Inning: Bobby Richardson, Mickey Mantle, Joe Pepitone*

Career High Season Batting Average — *1957 (.365)*

First Major League Home Run — *May 1, 1951; Left-handed*

Last Major League Home Run — *#536, September 20, 1968; Left-handed*

More Walks than Hits, Season, AL — *1962: BB 122, H 121, BA .321; 1968: BB 106, H 103, BA .237*

Most Combined Hits and Walks, Season, AL — *1956: H 188, BB 122, Total 300; 1957: H 173, BB 146, Total 319*

Career Spent with One Team — *NY Yankees, 18 years*

Most Home Runs Hit Against (Team) — *1. Washington Senators (80); 2. Detroit Tigers (74); 3. Chicago White Sox (73); 4. Boston Red Sox (69); 5. Cleveland Indians (64)*

Most Home Runs Hit Against (Pitcher) — *1. Early Wynn (13); 2. Pedro Ramos (12); 3. Camilo Pascual (11); 4. Frank Lary (9); 5. (Tie) Chuck Stobbs, Dick Donovan, Billy Pierce, Gary Bell (8)*

Home Runs

Mickey Mantle's 536 Regular Season Home Runs

1951

1. May 1, 1951, Comiskey Park vs. Chicago White Sox
2. May 4, 1951, Sportsman's Park vs. St. Louis Browns
3. May 13, 1951, Shibe Park vs. Philadelphia A's
4. May 16, 1951, Yankee Stadium vs. Cleveland Indians
5. June 19, 1951, Yankee Stadium vs. Chicago White Sox
6. June 19, 1951, Yankee Stadium vs. Chicago White Sox
7. July 7, 1951, Fenway Park vs. Boston Red Sox
8. August 25, 1951, Municipal Stadium vs. Cleveland Indians
9. August 29, 1951, Sportsman's Park vs. St. Louis Browns
10. September 8, 1951, Yankee Stadium vs. Washington Senators
11. September 9, 1951, Yankee Stadium vs. Washington Senators
12. September 12, 1951, Yankee Stadium vs. Detroit Tigers
13. September 19, 1951, Yankee Stadium vs. Chicago White Sox

1952

14. April 21, 1952, Yankee Stadium vs. Philadelphia A's
15. April 30, 1952, Yankee Stadium vs. St. Louis Browns
16. May 30, 1952, Yankee Stadium vs. Philadelphia A's
17. June 15, 1952, Municipal Stadium vs. Cleveland Indians
18. June 17, 1952, Briggs Stadium vs. Detroit Tigers
19. June 22, 1952, Comiskey Park vs. Chicago White Sox
20. June 27, 1952, Yankee Stadium vs. Philadelphia A's
21. July 5, 1952, Shibe Park vs. Philadelphia A's
22. July 6, 1952, Shibe Park vs. Philadelphia A's
23. July 13, 1952, Yankee Stadium vs. Detroit Tigers
24. July 13, 1952, Yankee Stadium vs. Detroit Tigers
25. July 15, 1952, Yankee Stadium vs. Cleveland Indians
26. July 17, 1952 Yankee Stadium vs. Cleveland Indians
27. July 25, 1952, Briggs Stadium vs. Detroit Tigers
28. July 26, 1952, Briggs Stadium vs. Detroit Tigers
29. July 29, 1952, Comiskey Park vs. Chicago White Sox
30. August 11, 1952, Yankee Stadium vs. Boston Red Sox
31. August 11, 1952, Yankee Stadium vs. Boston Red Sox
32. August 30, 1952, Yankee Stadium vs. Washington Senators
33. September 14, 1952, Municipal Stadium vs. Cleveland Indians
34. September 17, 1952, Briggs Stadium vs. Detroit Tigers
35. September 24, 1952, Fenway Park vs. Boston Red Sox
36. September 26, 1952, Shibe Park vs. Philadelphia A's

1953

37. April 17, 1953, Griffith Stadium vs. Washington Senators
38. April 23, 1953, Yankee Stadium vs. Boston Red Sox

39.   April 28, 1953, Busch Stadium vs. St. Louis Browns
40.   April 30, 1953, Comiskey Park vs. Chicago White Sox
41.   May 9, 1953, Fenway Park vs. Boston Red Sox
42.   May 25, 1953, Yankee Stadium vs. Boston Red Sox
43.   June 4, 1953, Comiskey Park vs. Chicago White Sox
44.   June 5, 1953, Busch Stadium vs. St. Louis Browns
45.   June 11, 1953, Briggs Stadium vs. Detroit Tigers
46.   June 18, 1953, Yankee Stadium vs. St. Louis Browns
47.   June 21, 1953, Yankee Stadium vs. Detroit Tigers
48.   June 23, 1953, Yankee Stadium vs. Chicago White Sox
49.   July 16, 1953, Connie Mack Stadium vs. Philadelphia A's
50.   July 26, 1953, Briggs Stadium vs. Detroit Tigers
51.   July 26, 1953, Briggs Stadium vs. Detroit Tigers
52.   August 7, 1953, Yankee Stadium vs. Chicago White Sox
53.   September 1, 1953, Comiskey Park vs. Chicago White Sox
54.   September 7, 1953, Fenway Park vs. Boston Red Sox
55.   September 9, 1953, Yankee Stadium vs. Chicago White Sox
56.   September 12, 1953, Yankee Stadium vs. Detroit Tigers
57.   September 20, 1953, Fenway Park vs. Boston Red Sox

1954

58.   April 19, 1954, Fenway Park vs. Boston Red Sox
59.   April 21, 1954, Yankee Stadium vs. Boston Red Sox
60.   May 7, 1954, Yankee Stadium vs. Philadelphia A's
61.   May 21, 1954, Yankee Stadium vs. Boston Red Sox
62.   May 22, 1954, Yankee Stadium vs. Boston Red Sox
63.   May 23, 1954, Yankee Stadium vs. Boston Red Sox
64.   May 25, 1954, Griffith Stadium vs. Washington Senators
65.   May 29, 1954, Fenway Park vs. Boston Red Sox
66.   May 30, 1954, Fenway Park vs. Boston Red Sox
67.   June 6, 1954, Yankee Stadium vs. Baltimore Orioles
68.   June 10, 1954, Yankee Stadium vs. Detroit Tigers
69.   June 20, 1954, Comiskey Park vs. Chicago White Sox
70.   June 26, 1954, Municipal Stadium vs. Cleveland Indians
71.   June 30, 1954, Fenway Park vs. Boston Red Sox
72.   July 1, 1954, Fenway Park vs. Boston Red Sox
73.   July 3, 1954, Yankee Stadium vs. Washington Senators
74.   July 5, 1954, Connie Mack Stadium vs. Philadelphia A's
75.   July 7, 1954, Yankee Stadium vs. Boston Red Sox
76.   July 19, 1954, Yankee Stadium vs. Detroit Tigers
77.   July 22, 1954, Yankee Stadium vs. Chicago White Sox
78.   July 28, 1954, Comiskey Park vs. Chicago White Sox
79.   August 5, 1954, Municipal Stadium vs. Cleveland Indians
80.   August 5, 1954, Municipal Stadium vs. Cleveland Indians
81.   August 8, 1954, Briggs Stadiums vs. Detroit Tigers
82.   August 12, 1954, Yankee Stadium vs. Philadelphia A's
83.   August 15, 1954, Yankee Stadium vs. Boston Red Sox
84.   September 2, 1954, Yankee Stadium vs. Cleveland Indians

1955

85.   April 13, 1955, Yankee Stadium vs. Washington Senators
86.   April 18, 1955, Memorial Stadium vs. Baltimore Orioles
87.   April 28, 1955, Municipal Stadium vs. Kansas City A's
88.   May 3, 1955, Municipal Stadium vs. Cleveland Indians
89.   May 6, 1955, Fenway Park vs. Boston Red Sox
90.   May 7, 1955, Fenway Park vs. Boston Red Sox
91.   May 11, 1955, Yankee Stadium vs. Cleveland Indians

92. May 13, 1955, Yankee Stadium vs. Detroit Tigers
93. May 13, 1955, Yankee Stadium vs. Detroit Tigers
94. May 13, 1955, Yankee Stadium vs. Detroit Tigers
95. May 18, 1955, Yankee Stadium vs. Chicago White Sox
96. June 3, 1955, Comiskey Park vs. Chicago White Sox
97. June 5, 1955, Comiskey Park vs. Chicago White Sox
98. June 6, 1955, Briggs Stadium vs. Detroit Tigers
99. June 17, 1955, Yankee Stadium vs. Chicago White Sox
100. June 19, 1955, Yankee Stadium vs. Chicago White Sox
101. June 21, 1955, Yankee Stadium vs. Kansas City A's
102. June 22, 1955, Yankee Stadium vs. Kansas City A's
103. July 10, 1955, Griffith Stadium vs. Washington Senators
104. July 10, 1955, Griffith Stadium vs. Washington Senators
105. July 10, 1955, Griffith Stadium vs. Washington Senators
106. July 28, 1955, Yankee Stadium vs. Chicago White Sox
107. July 31, 1955, Yankee Stadium vs. Kansas City A's
108. August 4, 1955, Yankee Stadium vs. Cleveland Indians
109. August 7, 1955, Yankee Stadium vs. Detroit Tigers
110. August 7, 1955, Yankee Stadium vs. Detroit Tigers
111. August 14, 1955, Memorial Stadium vs. Baltimore Orioles
112. August 15, 1955, Memorial Stadium vs. Baltimore Orioles
113. August 15, 1955, Memorial Stadium vs. Baltimore Orioles
114. August 16, 1955, Fenway Park vs. Boston Red Sox
115. August 19, 1955, Yankee Stadium vs. Baltimore Orioles
116. August 21, 1955, Yankee Stadium vs. Baltimore Orioles
117. August 24, 1955, Briggs Stadium vs. Detroit Tigers
118. August 28, 1955, Comiskey Park vs. Chicago White Sox
119. August 31, 1955, Municipal Stadium vs. Kansas City A's
120. September 2, 1955, Yankee Stadium vs. Washington Senators
121. September 4, 1955, Yankee Stadium vs. Washington Senators

1956
122. April 17, 1956, Griffith Stadium vs. Washington Senators
123. April 17, 1956, Griffith Stadium vs. Washington Senators
124. April 20, 1956, Yankee Stadium vs. Boston Red Sox
125. April 21, 1956, Yankee Stadium vs. Boston Red Sox
126. May 1 1956, Yankee Stadium vs. Detroit Tigers
127. May 2, 1956, Yankee Stadium vs. Detroit Tigers
128. May 3, 1956, Yankee Stadium vs. Kansas City A's
129. May 5, 1956, Yankee Stadium vs. Kansas City A's
130. May 5, 1956, Yankee Stadium vs. Kansas City A's
131. May 8, 1956, Yankee Stadium vs. Cleveland Indians
132. May 10, 1956, Yankee Stadium vs. Cleveland Indians
133. May 14, 1956, Municipal Stadium vs. Cleveland Indians
134. May 16, 1956, Municipal Stadium vs. Cleveland Indians
135. May 18, 1956, Comiskey Park vs. Chicago White Sox
136. May 18, 1956, Comiskey Park vs. Chicago White Sox
137. May 21, 1956, Municipal Stadium vs. Kansas City A's
138. May 24, 1956, Briggs Stadium vs. Detroit Tigers
139. May 29, 1956, Yankee Stadium vs. Boston Red Sox
140. May 30, 1956, Yankee Stadium vs. Washington Senators
141. May 30, 1956, Yankee Stadium vs. Washington Senators
142. June 5, 1956, Yankee Stadium vs. Kansas City A's
143. June 14, 1956, Yankee Stadium vs. Chicago White Sox
144. June 15, 1956, Municipal Stadium vs. Cleveland Indians
145. June 16, 1956, Municipal Stadium vs. Cleveland Indians
146. June 18, 1956, Briggs Stadium vs. Detroit Tigers

147.   June 20, 1956, Briggs Stadium vs. Detroit Tigers
148.   June 20, 1956, Briggs Stadium vs. Detroit Tigers
149.   July 1, 1956, Yankee Stadium vs. Washington Senators
150.   July 1, 1956, Yankee Stadium vs. Washington Senators
151.   July 14, 1956, Yankee Stadium vs. Cleveland Indians
152.   July 18, 1956, Yankee Stadium vs. Detroit Tigers
153.   July 22, 1956, Yankee Stadium vs. Kansas City A's
154.   July 30, 1956, Municipal Stadium vs. Cleveland Indians
155.   July 30, 1956, Municipal Stadium vs. Cleveland Indians
156.   August 4, 1956, Briggs Stadium vs. Detroit Tigers
157.   August 4, 1956, Briggs Stadium vs. Detroit Tigers
158.   August 5, 1956, Briggs Stadium vs. Detroit Tigers
159.   August 8, 1956, Griffith Stadium vs. Washington Senators
160.   August 9, 1956, Griffith Stadium vs. Washington Senators
161.   August 11, 1956, Yankee Stadium vs. Baltimore Orioles
162.   August 12, 1956, Yankee Stadium vs. Baltimore Orioles
163.   August 14, 1956, Yankee Stadium vs. Boston Red Sox
164.   August 23, 1956, Yankee Stadium vs. Chicago White Sox
165.   August 25, 1956, Yankee Stadium vs. Chicago White Sox
166.   August 28, 1956, Yankee Stadium vs. Kansas City A's
167.   August 29, 1956, Yankee Stadium vs. Kansas City A's
168.   August 31, 1956, Griffith Stadium vs. Washington Senators
169.   September 13, 1956, Municipal Stadium vs. Kansas City A's
170.   September 16, 1956, Municipal Stadium vs. Cleveland Indians
171.   September 18, 1956, Comiskey Park vs. Chicago White Sox
172.   September 21, 1956, Fenway Park vs. Boston Red Sox
173.   September 28, 1956, Yankee Stadium vs. Boston Red Sox

1957
174.   April 22, 1957, Griffith Stadium vs. Washington Senators
175.   April 24, 1957, Yankee Stadium vs. Baltimore Orioles
176.   May 5, 1957, Comiskey Park vs. Chicago White Sox
177.   May 8, 1957, Municipal Stadium vs. Cleveland Indians
178.   May 12, 1957, Memorial Stadium vs. Baltimore Orioles
179.   May 16, 1957, Yankee Stadium vs. Kansas City A's
180.   May 19, 1957, Yankee Stadium vs. Cleveland Indians
181.   May 25, 1957, Yankee Stadium vs. Washington Senators
182.   May 26, 1957, Yankee Stadium vs. Washington Senators
183.   May 29, 1957, Griffith Stadium vs. Washington Senators
184.   June 2, 1957, Yankee Stadium vs. Baltimore Orioles
185.   June 5, 1957, Municipal Stadium vs. Cleveland Indians
186.   June 6, 1957, Municipal Stadium vs. Cleveland Indians
187.   June 7, 1957, Briggs Stadium vs. Detroit Tigers
188.   June 10, 1957, Briggs Stadium vs. Detroit Tigers
189.   June 11, 1957, Comiskey Park vs. Chicago White Sox
190.   June 12, 1957, Comiskey Park vs. Chicago White Sox
191.   June 12, 1957, Comiskey Park vs. Chicago White Sox
192.   June 14, 1957, Municipal Stadium vs. Kansas City A's
193.   June 22, 1957, Yankee Stadium vs. Chicago White Sox
194.   June 23, 1957, Yankee Stadium vs. Chicago White Sox
195.   July 1, 1957, Memorial Stadium vs. Baltimore Orioles
196.   July 11, 1957, Municipal Stadium vs. Kansas City A's
197.   July 12, 1957, Municipal Stadium vs. Kansas City A's
198.   July 21, 1957, Municipal Stadium vs. Kansas City A's
199.   July 23, 1957, Yankee Stadium vs. Chicago White Sox
200.   July 26, 1957, Yankee Stadium vs. Detroit Tigers
201.   July 31, 1957, Yankee Stadium vs. Kansas City A's

202. August 2, 1957, Yankee Stadium vs. Cleveland Indians
203. August 7, 1957, Yankee Stadium vs. Washington Senators
204. August 10, 1957, Memorial Stadium vs. Baltimore Orioles
205. August 13, 1957, Fenway Park vs. Boston Red Sox
206. August 26, 1957, Briggs Stadium vs. Detroit Tigers
207. August 30, 1957, Yankee Stadium vs. Washington Senators

1958
208. April 17, 1958, Fenway Park vs. Boston Red Sox
209. May 9, 1958, Yankee Stadium vs. Washington Senators
210. May 18, 1958, Griffith Stadium vs. Washington Senators
211. May 20, 1958, Comiskey Park vs. Chicago White Sox
212. June 2, 1958, Yankee Stadium vs. Chicago White Sox
213. June 3, 1958, Yankee Stadium vs. Chicago White Sox
214. June 4, 1958, Yankee Stadium vs. Chicago White Sox
215. June 5, 1958, Yankee Stadium vs. Chicago White Sox
216. June 6, 1958, Yankee Stadium vs. Cleveland Indians
217. June 6, 1958, Yankee Stadium vs. Cleveland Indians
218. June 8, 1958, Yankee Stadium vs. Cleveland Indians
219. June 13, 1958, Yankee Stadium vs. Detroit Tigers
220. June 24, 1958, Comiskey Park vs. Chicago White Sox
221. June 29, 1958, Municipal Stadium vs. Kansas City A's
222. July 1, 1958, Memorial Stadium vs. Baltimore Orioles
223. July 1, 1958, Memorial Stadium vs. Baltimore Orioles
224. July 3, 1958, Griffith Stadium vs. Washington Senators
225. July 3, 1958, Griffith Stadium vs. Washington Senators
226. July 4, 1958, Griffith Stadium vs. Washington Senators
227. July 5, 1958, Yankee Stadium vs. Boston Red Sox
228. July 6, 1958, Yankee Stadium vs. Boston Red Sox
229. July 11, 1958, Yankee Stadium vs. Cleveland Indians
230. July 14, 1958, Yankee Stadium vs. Chicago White Sox
231. July 15, 1958, Yankee Stadium vs. Detroit Tigers
232. July 23, 1958, Briggs Stadium vs. Detroit Tigers
233. July 24, 1958, Briggs Stadium vs. Detroit Tigers
234. July 28, 1958, Municipal Stadium vs. Kansas City A's
235. July 28, 1958, Municipal Stadium vs. Kansas City A's
236. August 4, 1958, Memorial Stadium vs. Baltimore Orioles
237. August 5, 1958, Memorial Stadium vs. Baltimore Orioles
238. August 9, 1958, Yankee Stadium vs. Boston Red Sox
239. August 11, 1958, Yankee Stadium vs. Baltimore Orioles
240. August 12, 1958, Yankee Stadium vs. Baltimore Orioles
241. August 16, 1958, Fenway Park vs. Boston Red Sox
242. August 17, 1958, Fenway Park vs. Boston Red Sox
243. August 22, 1958, Yankee Stadium vs. Chicago White Sox
244. August 27, 1958, Yankee Stadium vs. Kansas City A's
245. September 2, 1958, Yankee Stadium vs. Boston Red Sox
246. September 3, 1958, Yankee Stadium vs. Boston Red Sox
247. September 9, 1958, Municipal Stadium vs. Cleveland Indians
248. September 17, 1958, Briggs Stadium vs. Detroit Tigers
249. September 24, 1958, Fenway Park vs. Boston Red Sox

1959
250. April 21, 1959, Griffith Stadium vs. Washington Senators
251. April 23, 1959, Griffith Stadium vs. Washington Senators
252. April 29, 1959, Comiskey Park vs. Chicago White Sox
253. May 10, 1959, Yankee Stadium vs. Washington Senators
254. May 12, 1959, Yankee Stadium vs. Cleveland Indians

255.   May 20, 1959, Yankee Stadium vs. Detroit Tigers
256.   May 23, 1959, Memorial Stadium vs. Baltimore Orioles
257.   May 24, 1959, Memorial Stadium vs. Baltimore Orioles
258.   May 30, 1959, Griffith Stadium vs. Washington Senators
259.   June 3, 1959, Briggs Stadium vs. Detroit Tigers
260.   June 9, 1959, Yankee Stadium vs. Kansas City A's
261.   June 11, 1959, Yankee Stadium vs. Kansas City A's
252.   June 13, 1959, Yankee Stadium vs. Detroit Tigers
263.   June 17, 1959, Yankee Stadium vs. Chicago White Sox
264.   June 18, 1959, Yankee Stadium vs. Chicago White Sox
265.   June 22, 1959, Municipal Stadium vs. Kansas City A's
266.   June 22, 1959, Municipal Stadium vs. Kansas City A's
267.   June 23, 1959, Municipal Stadium vs. Kansas City A's
268.   July 16, 1959, Yankee Stadium vs. Cleveland Indians
269.   July 19, 1959, Yankee Stadium vs. Chicago White Sox
270.   August 4, 1959, Yankee Stadium vs. Detroit Tigers
271.   August 5, 1959, Yankee Stadium vs. Detroit Tigers
272.   August 16, 1959, Yankee Stadium vs. Boston Red Sox
273.   August 16, 1959, Yankee Stadium vs. Boston Red Sox
274.   August 26, 1959, Municipal Stadium vs. Cleveland Indians
275.   August 29, 1959, Griffith Stadium vs. Washington Senators
276.   September 7, 1959, Fenway Park vs. Boston Red Sox
277.   September 10, 1959, Yankee Stadium vs. Kansas City A's
278.   September 13, 1959, Yankee Stadium vs. Cleveland Indians
279.   September 15, 1959, Yankee Stadium vs. Chicago White Sox
280.   September 15, 1959, Yankee Stadium vs. Chicago White Sox

1960
281.   April 22, 1960, Yankee Stadium vs. Baltimore Orioles
282.   May 13, 1960, Griffith Stadium vs. Washington Senators
283.   May 17, 1960, Municipal Stadium vs. Cleveland Indians
284.   May 20, 1960, Comiskey Park vs. Chicago White Sox
285.   May 29, 1960, Yankee Stadium vs. Washington Senators
286.   May 29, 1960, Yankee Stadium vs. Washington Senators
287.   June 1, 1960, Memorial Stadium vs. Baltimore Orioles
288.   June 5, 1960, Yankee Stadium vs. Boston Red Sox
289.   June 8, 1960, Yankee Stadium vs. Chicago White Sox
290.   June 8, 1960, Yankee Stadium vs. Chicago White Sox
291.   June 9, 1960, Yankee Stadium vs. Chicago White Sox
292.   June 10, 1960, Yankee Stadium vs. Cleveland Indians
293.   June 17, 1960, Comiskey Park vs. Chicago White Sox
294.   June 18, 1960, Comiskey Park vs. Chicago White Sox
295.   June 21, 1960, Briggs Stadium vs. Detroit Tigers
296.   June 21, 1960, Briggs Stadium vs. Detroit Tigers
297.   June 28, 1960, Yankee Stadium vs. Kansas City A's
298.   June 30, 1960, Yankee Stadium vs. Kansas City A's
299.   July 3, 1960, Yankee Stadium vs. Detroit Tigers
300.   July 4, 1960, Griffith Stadium vs. Washington Senators
301.   July 15, 1960, Briggs Stadium vs. Detroit Tigers
302.   July 18, 1960, Municipal Stadium vs. Cleveland Indians
303.   July 20, 1960, Municipal Stadium vs. Cleveland Indians
304.   July 24, 1960, Yankee Stadium vs. Chicago White Sox
305.   July 26, 1960, Yankee Stadium vs. Cleveland Indians
306.   July 28, 1960, Yankee Stadium vs. Cleveland Indians
307.   July 31, 1960, Yankee Stadium vs. Kansas City A's
308.   August 15, 1960, Yankee Stadium vs. Baltimore Orioles
309.   August 15, 1960, Yankee Stadium vs. Baltimore Orioles

310. August 26, 1960, Yankee Stadium vs. Cleveland Indians
311. August 28, 1960, Yankee Stadium vs. Detroit Tigers
312. September 6, 1960, Yankee Stadium vs. Boston Red Sox
313. September 10, 1960, Briggs Stadium vs. Detroit Tigers
314. September 11, 1960, Municipal Stadium vs. Cleveland Indians
315. September 17, 1960, Yankee Stadium vs. Baltimore Orioles
316. September 20, 1960, Yankee Stadium vs. Washington Senators
317. September 21, 1960, Yankee Stadium vs. Washington Senators
318. September 24, 1960, Fenway Park vs. Boston Red Sox
319. September 28, 1960, Griffith Stadium vs. Washington Senators
320. September 28, 1960, Griffith Stadium vs. Washington Senators

1961

321. April 17, 1961, Yankee Stadium vs. Kansas City A's
322. April 20, 1961, Yankee Stadium vs. Los Angeles Angels
323. April 20, 1961, Yankee Stadium vs. Los Angeles Angels
324. April 21, 1961, Memorial Stadium vs. Baltimore Orioles
325. April 23, 1961, Memorial Stadium vs. Baltimore Orioles
326. April 26, 1961, Tiger Stadium vs. Detroit Tigers
327. April 26, 1961, Tiger Stadium vs. Detroit Tigers
328. May 2, 1961, Metropolitan Stadium vs. Minnesota Twins
329. May 4, 1961, Metropolitan Stadium vs. Minnesota Twins
330. May 16, 1961, Yankee Stadium vs. Washington Senators
331. May 29, 1961, Fenway Park vs. Boston Red Sox
332. May 30, 1961, Fenway Park vs. Boston Red Sox
333. May 30, 1961, Fenway Park vs. Boston Red Sox
334. May 31, 1961, Fenway Park vs. Boston Red Sox
335. June 5, 1961, Yankee Stadium vs. Minnesota Twins
336. June 9, 1961, Yankee Stadium vs. Kansas City A's
337. June 10, 1961, Yankee Stadium vs. Kansas City A's
338. June 11, 1961, Yankee Stadium vs. Los Angeles Angels
339. June 15, 1961, Municipal Stadium vs. Cleveland Indians
340. June 17, 1961, Tiger Stadium vs. Detroit Tigers
341. June 21, 1961, Municipal Stadium vs. Kansas City A's
342. June 21, 1961, Municipal Stadium vs. Kansas City A's
343. June 26, 1961, Wrigley Field vs. Los Angeles Angels
344. June 28, 1961, Wrigley Field vs. Los Angeles Angels
345. June 30, 1961, Yankee Stadium vs. Washington Senators
346. July 1, 1961, Yankee Stadium vs. Washington Senators
347. July 1, 1961, Yankee Stadium vs. Washington Senators
348. July 2, 1961, Yankee Stadium vs. Washington Senators
349. July 8, 1961, Yankee Stadium vs. Boston Red Sox
350. July 13, 1961, Comiskey Park vs. Chicago White Sox
351. July 14, 1961, Comiskey Park vs. Chicago White Sox
352. July 16, 1961, Memorial Stadium vs. Baltimore Orioles
353. July 17, 1961, Memorial Stadium vs. Baltimore Orioles
354. July 18, 1961, Griffith Stadium vs. Washington Senators
355. July 18, 1961, Griffith Stadium vs. Washington Senators
356. July 19, 1961, Griffith Stadium vs. Washington Senators
357. July 21, 1961, Fenway Park vs. Boston Red Sox
358. July 25, 1961, Yankee Stadium vs. Chicago White Sox
359. July 26, 1961, Yankee Stadium vs. Chicago White Sox
360. August 2, 1961, Yankee Stadium vs. Kansas City A's
361. August 6, 1961, Yankee Stadium vs. Minnesota Twins
362. August 6, 1961, Yankee Stadium vs. Minnesota Twins
363. August 6, 1961, Yankee Stadium vs. Minnesota Twins
364. August 11, 1961, Yankee Stadium vs. Washington Senators

365. August 13, 1961, Griffith Stadium vs. Washington Senators
366. August 20, 1961, Municipal Stadium vs. Cleveland Indians
367. August 30, 1961, Metropolitan Stadium vs. Minnesota Twins
368. August 31, 1961, Metropolitan Stadium vs. Minnesota Twins
369. September 3, 1961, Yankee Stadium vs. Detroit Tigers
370. September 3, 1961, Yankee Stadium vs. Detroit Tigers
371. September 5, 1961, Yankee Stadium vs. Washington Senators
372. September 8, 1961, Yankee Stadium vs. Cleveland Indians
373. September 10, 1961, Yankee Stadium vs. Cleveland Indians
374. September 23, 1961, Fenway Park vs. Boston Red Sox

1962

375. April 10, 1962, Yankee Stadium vs. Baltimore Orioles
376. April 19, 1962, Memorial Stadium vs. Baltimore Orioles
377. May 5, 1962, Yankee Stadium vs. Washington Senators
378. May 6, 1962, Yankee Stadium vs. Washington Senators
379. May 6, 1962, Yankee Stadium vs. Washington Senators
380. May 6, 1962, Yankee Stadium vs. Washington Senators
381. May 12, 1962, Municipal Stadium vs. Cleveland Indians
382. June 16, 1962, Municipal Stadium vs. Cleveland Indians
383. June 23, 1962, Tiger Stadium vs. Detroit Tigers
384. June 28, 1962, Yankee Stadium vs. Minnesota Twins
385. July 2, 1962, Yankee Stadium vs. Kansas City A's
386. July 3, 1962, Yankee Stadium vs. Kansas City A's
387. July 3, 1962, Yankee Stadium vs. Kansas City A's
388. July 4, 1962, Yankee Stadium vs. Kansas City A's
389. July 4, 1962, Yankee Stadium vs. Kansas City A's
390. July 6, 1962, Metropolitan Stadium vs. Minnesota Twins
391. July 6, 1962, Metropolitan Stadium vs. Minnesota Twins
392. July 18, 1962, Fenway Park vs. Boston Red Sox
393. July 20, 1962, Yankee Stadium vs. Washington Senators
394. July 25, 1962, Yankee Stadium vs. Boston Red Sox
395. July 28, 1962, Yankee Stadium vs. Chicago White Sox
396. August 17, 1962, Municipal Stadium vs. Kansas City A's
397. August 18, 1962, Municipal Stadium vs. Kansas City A's
398. August 19, 1962, Municipal Stadium vs. Kansas City A's
399. August 28, 1962, Yankee Stadium vs. Cleveland Indians
400. September 10, 1962, Tiger Stadium vs. Detroit Tigers
401. September 12, 1962, Municipal Stadium vs. Cleveland Indians
402. September 18, 1962, D.C. Stadium vs. Washington Senators
403. September 18, 1962, D.C. Stadium vs. Washington Senators
404. September 30, 1962, Yankee Stadium vs. Chicago White Sox

1963

405. April 10, 1963, Municipal Stadium vs. Kansas City A's
406. April 11, 1963, Yankee Stadium vs. Baltimore Orioles
407. May 4, 1963, Metropolitan Stadium vs. Minnesota Twins
408. May 6, 1963, Tiger Stadium vs. Detroit Tigers
409. May 11, 1963, Memorial Stadium vs. Baltimore Orioles
410. May 15, 1963, Yankee Stadium vs. Minnesota Twins
411. May 21, 1963, Yankee Stadium vs. Kansas City A's
412. May 21, 1963, Yankee Stadium vs. Kansas City A's
413. May 22, 1963, Yankee Stadium vs. Kansas City A's
414. May 26, 1963, Yankee Stadium vs. Washington Senators
415. June 4, 1963, Memorial Stadium vs. Baltimore Orioles
416. August 4, 1963, Yankee Stadium vs. Baltimore Orioles
417. September 1, 1963, Memorial Stadium vs. Baltimore Orioles

418. September 11, 1963, Municipal Stadium vs. Kansas City A's
419. September 21, 1963, Yankee Stadium vs. Kansas City A's

1964
420. May 6, 1964, D.C. Stadium vs. Washington Senators
421. May 6, 1964, D.C. Stadium vs. Washington Senators
422. May 8, 1964, Municipal Stadium vs. Cleveland Indians
423. May 9, 1964, Municipal Stadium vs. Cleveland Indians
424. May 16, 1964, Yankee Stadium vs. Kansas City A's
425. May 17, 1964, Yankee Stadium vs. Kansas City A's
426. May 23, 1964, Yankee Stadium vs. Los Angeles Angels
427. May 24, 1964, Yankee Stadium vs. Los Angeles Angels
428. June 11, 1964, Fenway Park vs. Boston Red Sox
429. June 11, 1964, Fenway Park vs. Boston Red Sox
430. June 13, 1964, Yankee Stadium vs. Chicago White Sox
431. June 17, 1964, Yankee Stadium vs. Boston Red Sox
432. June 21, 1964, Comiskey Park vs. Chicago White Sox
433. June 23, 1964, Memorial Stadium vs. Baltimore Orioles
434. June 27, 1964, Yankee Stadium vs. Detroit Tigers
435. July 1, 1964, Yankee Stadium vs. Kansas City A's
436. July 4, 1964, Yankee Stadium vs. Minnesota Twins
437. July 13, 1964, Municipal Stadium vs. Cleveland Indians
438. July 24, 1964, Tiger Stadium vs. Detroit Tigers
439. July 28, 1964, Chavez Ravine vs. Los Angeles Angels
440. August 1, 1964, Metropolitan Stadium vs. Minnesota Twins
441. August 4, 1964, Municipal Stadium vs. Kansas City A's
442. August 11, 1964, Yankee Stadium vs. Chicago White Sox
443. August 12, 1964, Yankee Stadium vs. Chicago White Sox
444. August 12, 1964, Yankee Stadium vs. Chicago White Sox
445. August 22, 1964, Fenway Park vs. Boston Red Sox
446. August 23, 1964, Fenway Park vs. Boston Red Sox
447. August 29, 1964, Yankee Stadium vs. Boston Red Sox
448. September 4, 1964, Municipal Stadium vs. Kansas City A's
449. September 5, 1964, Municipal Stadium vs. Kansas City A's
450. September 17, 1964, Yankee Stadium vs. Los Angeles Angels
451. September 19, 1964, Yankee Stadium vs. Kansas City A's
452. September 22, 1964, Municipal Stadium vs. Cleveland Indians
453. September 27, 1964, D.C. Stadium vs. Washington Senators
454. September 30, 1964, Yankee Stadium vs. Detroit Tigers

1965
455. April 17, 1965, Municipal Stadium vs. Kansas City A's
456. April 18, 1965, Municipal Stadium vs. Kansas City A's
457. April 21, 1965, Yankee Stadium vs. Minnesota Twins
458. April 25, 1965, Yankee Stadium vs. Los Angeles Angels
459. May 10, 1965, Fenway Park vs. Boston Red Sox
460. May 11, 1965, Fenway Park vs. Boston Red Sox
461. May 15, 1965, Memorial Stadium vs. Baltimore Orioles
462. May 30, 1965, Comiskey Park vs. Chicago White Sox
463. June 5, 1965, Yankee Stadium vs. Chicago White Sox
464. June 18, 1965, Yankee Stadium vs. Minnesota Twins
465. June 22, 1965, Yankee Stadium vs. Kansas City A's
466. July 15, 1965, Yankee Stadium vs. Washington Senators
467. July 25, 1965, Municipal Stadium vs. Cleveland Indians
468. August 6, 1965, Tiger Stadium vs. Detroit Tigers
469. August 7, 1965, Tiger Stadium vs. Detroit Tigers
470. August 10, 1965, Yankee Stadium vs. Minnesota Twins

471.   August 18, 1965, Yankee Stadium vs. Los Angeles Angels
472.   September 2, 1965, Chavez Ravine vs. Los Angeles Angels
473.   September 4, 1965, Yankee Stadium vs. Boston Red Sox

1966
474.   May 9, 1966, Metropolitan Stadium vs. Minnesota Twins
475.   May 14, 1966, Municipal Stadium vs. Kansas City A's
476.   May 25, 1966, Yankee Stadium vs. California Angels
477.   May 25, 1966, Yankee Stadium vs. California Angels
478.   June 1, 1966, Comiskey Park vs. Chicago White Sox
479.   June 16, 1966, Yankee Stadium vs. Cleveland Indians
480.   June 23, 1966, Yankee Stadium vs. Baltimore Orioles
481.   June 28, 1966, Fenway Park vs. Boston Red Sox
482.   June 28, 1966, Fenway Park vs. Boston Red Sox
483.   June 29, 1966, Fenway Park vs. Boston Red Sox
484.   June 29, 1966, Fenway Park vs. Boston Red Sox
485.   July 1, 1966, D.C. Stadium vs. Washington Senators
486.   July 2, 1966, D.C. Stadium vs. Washington Senators
487.   July 2, 1966, D.C. Stadium vs. Washington Senators
488.   July 3, 1966, D.C. Stadium vs. Washington Senators
489.   July 7, 1966, Yankee Stadium vs. Boston Red Sox
490.   July 8, 1966, Yankee Stadium vs. Washington Senators
491.   July 8, 1966, Yankee Stadium vs. Washington Senators
492.   July 23, 1966, Yankee Stadium vs. California Angels
493.   July 24, 1966, Yankee Stadium vs. California Angels
494.   July 29, 1966, Comiskey Park vs. Chicago White Sox
495.   August 14, 1966, Yankee Stadium vs. Cleveland Indians
496.   August 26, 1966, Yankee Stadium vs. Detroit Tigers

1967
497.   April 29, 1967, Yankee Stadium vs. California Angels
498.   April 30,1967, Yankee Stadium vs. California Angels
499.   May 3, 1967, Metropolitan Stadium vs. Minnesota Twins
500.   May 14, 1967, Yankee Stadium vs. Baltimore Orioles
501.   May 17, 1967, Yankee Stadium vs. Cleveland Indians
502.   May 19, 1967, Tiger Stadium vs. Detroit Tigers
503.   May 20, 1967, Tiger Stadium vs. Detroit Tigers
504.   May 21, 1967, Tiger Stadium vs. Detroit Tigers
505.   May 24, 1967, Memorial Stadium vs. Baltimore Orioles
506.   May 27, 1967, Municipal Stadium vs. Cleveland Indians
507.   May 28, 1967, Municipal Stadium vs. Cleveland Indians
508.   June 5, 1967, Yankee Stadium vs. Washington Senators
509.   June 15, 1967, D.C. Stadium vs. Washington Senators
510.   June 24, 1967, Yankee Stadium vs. Detroit Tigers
511.   July 4, 1967, Metropolitan Stadium vs. Minnesota Twins
512.   July 4, 1967, Metropolitan Stadium vs. Minnesota Twins
513.   July 16, 1967, Yankee Stadium vs. Baltimore Orioles
514.   July 22, 1967, Tiger Stadium vs. Detroit Tigers
515.   July 25, 1967, Yankee Stadium vs. Minnesota Twins
516.   August 7, 1967, Anaheim Stadium vs. California Angels
517.   September 2, 1967, Yankee Stadium vs. Washington Senators
518.   September 3, 1967, Yankee Stadium vs. Washington Senators

1968
519.   April 18, 1968, Anaheim Stadium vs. California Angels
520.   April 24, 1968, Oakland Coliseum vs. Oakland A's
521.   April 26, 1968, Yankee Stadium vs. Detroit Tigers

522. May 6, 1968, Yankee Stadium vs. Cleveland Indians
523. May 30, 1968, Yankee Stadium vs. Washington Senators
524. May 30, 1968, Yankee Stadium vs. Washington Senators
525. June 7, 1968, Yankee Stadium vs. California Angels
526. June 11, 1968, Yankee Stadium vs. Chicago White Sox
527. June 16, 1968, Anaheim Stadium vs. California Angels
528. June 22, 1968, Metropolitan Stadium vs. Minnesota Twins
529. June 29, 1968, Yankee Stadium vs. Oakland A's
530. August 10, 1968, Yankee Stadium vs. Minnesota Twins
531. August 10, 1968, Yankee Stadium vs. Minnesota Twins
532. August 12, 1968, Anaheim Stadium vs. California Angels
533. August 15, 1968, Oakland Coliseum vs. Oakland A's
534. August 22, 1968, Metropolitan Stadium vs. Minnesota Twins
535. September 19, 1968, Tiger Stadium vs. Detroit Tigers
536. September 20, 1968, Yankee Stadium vs. Boston Red Sox

Total: Left-handed - 372, right-handed - 164

WORLD SERIES HOME RUNS

1. October 6, 1952, Ebbets Field vs. Brooklyn Dodgers
2. October 7, 1952, Ebbets Field vs. Brooklyn Dodgers
3. October 1, 1953, Yankee Stadium vs. Brooklyn Dodgers
4. October 4, 1953, Ebbets Field vs. Brooklyn Dodgers
5. September 30, 1955, Ebbets Field vs. Brooklyn Dodgers
6. October 3, 1956, Ebbets Field vs. Brooklyn Dodgers
7. October 7, 1956, Yankee Stadium vs. Brooklyn Dodgers
8. October 8, 1956, Yankee Stadium vs. Brooklyn Dodgers
9. October 5, 1957, County Stadium vs. Milwaukee Braves
10. October 2, 1958, County Stadium vs. Milwaukee Braves
11. October 2, 1958, County Stadium vs. Milwaukee Braves
12. October 6, 1960, Forbes Field vs. Pittsburgh Pirates
13. October 6, 1960, Forbes Field vs. Pittsburgh Pirates
14. October 8, 1960, Yankee Stadium vs. Pittsburgh Pirates
15. October 6, 1963, Dodger Stadium vs. Los Angeles Dodgers
16. October 10, 1964, Yankee Stadium vs. St. Louis Cardinals
17. October 14, 1964, Busch Stadium vs. St. Louis Cardinals
18. October 15, 1964, Busch Stadium vs. St. Louis Cardinals

Total: Left-handed - 10, right-handed - 8

ALL STAR GAME HOME RUNS

1. July 22, 1955, County Stadium, Milwaukee - Pitcher Robin Roberts
2. July 10, 1956, Griffith Stadium, Washington - Pitcher Warren Spahn

Total: Left-handed - 1, right-handed - 1

Mickey Mantle

October 20, 1931 — August 13, 1995

★ ★ ★ ★ ORDER FORM ★ ★ ★ ★

ITEM	PRICE	QTY	*SIZE	TOTAL
Mickey Mantle Video	$29.95		N/A	
Mickey Mantle Book	$29.95		N/A	
John Madden Video	$29.95		N/A	
Mickey Mantle Baseball Cap (Navy blue-4-color logo)	$17.95		N/A	
MM T-Shirt #1: Special Edition (White with Sepia photo)	$19.95			
MM Sweatshirt #1: Special Edition (White with Sepia photo)	$29.95			
MM T-shirt #2: American Dream (Navy blue with 4-color logo)	$19.95			
MM sweatshirt #2: American Dream (Navy blue with 4-color logo)	$29.95			
MM Embroidered Golf Shirt (Navy blue)	$49.95			

*Shirt Sizes L - XL - (XXL add $3.00)

SUBTOTAL:	$
California Residents add 8.25% **SALES TAX**	$
SHIPPING ($4.50 for 1st item, $2.50 for each additional item)	$
TOTAL	$

CUSTOMER INFORMATION

Name _____

Agency _____

Address _____

City _____

State _____ Zip _____

Phone (____) _____

METHOD OF PAYMENT:

Visa ____ MC ____ Check# _____

Acct# _____

Exp. date _____

Signature _____

To order, send check or money order to **Baseball Legend Video, Ltd.**, 1253 Vallejo St., San Francisco, CA 94109. Please allow 3-4 weeks for delivery. To order by fax, fax a copy of this order form, with credit card information and your signature.

To order by phone, call 1-800-THE MICK (1-800-843-6425).